"Pia's poems capture echoes from the past, reflections on the present and hope for the future. T.S. Eliot in "Four Quartets" writes:

> "Footfalls echo in the memory
> Down the passage that we did not take
> Towards the door we never opened
> Into the rose-garden"

The echoes from Pia's life as she reflects on the harsh realities of life's experiences and the disappointment of unfulfilled dreams can evoke our own echoes. But her poetry does more than dwell on life's disappointments; it also reveals the healing power of beauty glimpsed in nature and in life-affirming relationships. She moves from darkness to light; from despair to discovery and to the assured hope of the eternal "Rose Garden".

Robyn Claydon
Author/International speaker/Lecturer in Poetry/
Listed in the World's Who's Who of Women and the
Dictionary of Distinguished Leadership

"Great poems and perfect synesthesia (words and art)."

Koraljka
Artist and Illustrator

"I have found Pia's ("Spirituality") poetry to be consistent and life giving and I commend the work highly.

Her poems are almost Psalm-ic or Proverbial in the biblical sense. They often present a 'tension' which needs resolution, which comes to finalisation in the last stanza, bringing release and joy.

I consider this to be a valuable piece of work and I thank her for allowing me the privilege of critique."

Ralph Estherby
Author/Australian Army Chaplain/Director of Chaplaincy Australia/
Senior Pastor at Breakthrough (ACC) Church Hornsby

MY BEST POEMS

Complete Collection

© 2017 by Pia Horan-Gross

All rights reserved. No portion of this book may be reproduced, stored in a retrieval system, or transmitted in any form or by any means – electronic, mechanical, photocopy, recording, scanning, or other – except for brief quotations in critical reviews or articles, without the prior written permission of the author/self-publisher.

Unless otherwise noted, Scripture quotations are taken form the Holy Bible, New King James Version (NKJV) ®. Copyright © 1982 by Thomas Nelson. Used by permission. All rights reserved.

ISBN 978-0-6480135-0-1

Acknowledgements

I would like to mention the following persons, who played a role in encouraging me to move forward with the publishing process of this collection of poetry:

Robyn Claydon, woman extraordinaire, who read my whole collection in record time and provided valuable and multifaceted feedback; Pastor Ralph, a gifted man and spiritual mentor who found the time to read through Part 3 Spirituality and provide helpful feedback; Koraljka, my illustrator and just a lovely human being, Rachel Cox who lent a professional finish to my books and a joy to work with.

As well, thank you to my family, friends and acquaintances who politely put up with my obsessive ramblings about this collection, the challenge of self-publishing and my not infrequent moaning about this process and the snags along the way!

Last but not least, thanks go to my God, who has given me this gift and love of writing, the time and health to do it and a cute and comfy caravan, which enables me to withdraw from life and spend uninterrupted hours working and focussing on this writing task!
I feel truly blessed!

Table of Contents

Acknowledgements	v
Part 1	1
FOREWORD	3
A RARE VISITOR	5
AUTUMN	7
BUSY AS A BEE?	10
CELEBRATION OF LIGHT	12
EVENING DANCE	14
FIREFLIES	16
GREY SUMMER'S DAY	20
MERE WATCHING	21
MORE RAIN AHEAD	23
POETRY AGAIN	24
PREHISTORIC ERUPTION	25
SOUL BREATHING	27
SPRING MORNING	28
THE BUMBLING BUMBLE BEE	30
THE PERFECTION OF SILENCE	32
THE WALL OF STONES	33

Part 2	35
FOREWORD	37
A PRISTINE DAY	39
A SERIES OF BRIEF ENCOUNTERS	41
AN UNSURRENDERED HEART	44
AND I THOUGHT WE WERE FRIENDS!	45
AWAKENING	47
CARS PASSING	48
CAT AND MOUSE GAME	49
COCKROACHES	51
EMPTY	53
FAILED HARVEST	54
FEELING RAW	56
FOOL'S GOLD?	57
FRAGMENTS	58
FRIENDS	60
FUTURE RESPONSE	61
I KNOW	62
IMPROMPTU PERFORMANCE	64
JUST A DREAM	66
JUST FOR YOU	67
LIVING WITH UNEASINESS	69
LONGING	70
LOST DREAMS	72

MAKING A STAND	73
NO ONE TOLD ME BACK THEN	75
ODE TO A SOUL-MATE DREAM	76
PAIN	80
PLAYING WITH FIRE	81
PREDATOR	82
QUITTING	83
RED CARNATIONS	84
SECRET GARDEN	85
SIMPLY THANK YOU	87
SUBSTITUTES	89
TENTS DANCING	90
THE ALLY	92
THE APPENDIX	94
THE BIRTH	96
THE DIARY	98
THE GUARDIAN	101
THE IDOL	104
THE MASQUERADE	105
THE ROAD TO FREEDOM	107
THE TOXIC PARENT	109
TIME	111
TO WRITE POETRY	113
TOUCHED BY THE DIVINE	114

TRANSITION	117
TRUE VINE COMMUNITY	118
WAITING	121
WITHOUT A VOICE	122
YOU AND I	125
Part 3	127
FOREWORD	129
A PICTURE OF THE VINEYARD	131
ABIDING	133
ANCIENT MANUSCRIPTS DECLARE	134
BLEAK DAY	136
BLESSED	138
CAGES	139
CESSPOOL	141
CHAMELEON	143
COCOON	145
CONSTRICTION	147
CONTEMPLATING MORTALITY	148
CORRIDORS	151
COUNT BLUEBEARD	152
COVERINGS	154
DRIFTING	155
EASTER REFLECTIONS	156

EX NIHILO	158
EXPRESSING THE INEXPRESSIBLE	160
FAITH vs. EXPECTATIONS	162
FAITH	164
FIG LEAVES	166
FREE TO LOVE	167
GENESIS AGAIN	168
GOD'S RICHNESS	170
HAY AND STUBBLE	171
HE KNOWS	172
HIS GIFT	174
HIS TEMPLE	177
HOUSE OF MIRRORS	178
IN HIM	180
IN HIS SAFE KEEPING – AT LAST!	181
LIFE'S LEARNING	182
LIFE'S LINK	183
MIRRORS	184
MY BELOVED	186
MY SWITZERLAND	187
NECESSARY DISILLUSIONMENT	188
NEW WORLD	190
ON MY WAY TO WORK	192
OUR MAGNIFICENT DESTINY	194

PARADISE	195
PRAYER	197
PRISONS	198
RESTLESS	199
RISEN	200
SCAPEGOAT	201
SEA OF TEARS	203
SHELTER FROM THE STORM	205
SHUTDOWN	206
SIMPLICITY	208
SURVIVAL DEMANDS IT	209
THE ALTAR OF THE LIE	211
THE ARTFUL DODGER	213
THE DAM	214
THE FINAL VERDICT	215
THE GOLDEN CUP OF POISON	217
THE GREAT WEDDING FEAST	219
THE GREATEST GIFT OF ALL	220
THE IDEALIST	222
THE MEANING OF LIFE	224
THE MYTH OF SELF-SUFFICIENCY	226
THE ONE ESSENTIAL THING	228
THE PARABLE OF FIRE	230
THE RELIGIOUS SELF	232

THE TEMPLE	233
THE UNIVERSAL FOUNT	236
TIME ALONE	238
WAKING FROM STUPOR	239
AUTHOR WEBSITE DETAILS	241

Part 1

Celebrating

NATURE

Dramatic,
Enchanting,
Rejuvenating

FOREWORD

*"But ask the animals, and they will teach you,
or the birds in the sky, and they will tell you;
or speak to the earth, and it will teach you,
or let the fish in the sea inform you.
Which of all these does not know
that the hand of the LORD has done this?
In his hand is the life of every creature
and the breath of all mankind."
Job 12:7-10*

From a very young age, I developed a special love and sensitivity to the natural world around me. As a five year old, I would eagerly seek out seasonal flowers and fruit, growing all around me, some in secluded, hidden places, in forests and fields, near singing creeks. They were a special delight to me. For six years, I lived in a tiny Swiss village called Seseglio, near the Italian border. For many years after, having moved away from that area, I pined for those memories.

For a long time, I was convinced that peace could only be found by seeking out nature. This proved in part true and nature continues to have a soothing influence upon me. I believe this applies to you also my reader, or you would not have chosen this book.

Only since discovering or literally stumbling over nature's Maker (sorry, not Mother Nature), nature has taken on a transcendental quality and role for me and contemplation of nature now equates to contemplation of its Maker. I often marvel at the abounding generosity of God, his humour and love of creativity, when I look at some of his quirky creative expressions, and at his goodness; as one minister would exclaim: "God is good because he created mangoes!"- and so much more! Finally, nature like mankind has become marred since its original conception and it is easy to lose sight of the inherent perfection in nature. Has it all become uncontrollable? To some extent yes, but not irreparably so.

That is my unshakable hope and belief; based on trustworthy promises, made by One who set all this in motion, a very long time ago, but not so long as to eclipse his origin and our destiny: eternity! That is his call for us and creation itself!

P.H.-G.

A RARE VISITOR

Today,
I heard that sound again:
Currawong call,
Magpie chatter,
Kookaburra laughter–
all in one!

Once again,
our timid visitor
paying us a rare visit.
A privilege indeed!
Its timing–
a mystery!

That long draping tail
spotted first.
Its plumage-
difficult to see in the scrub.
What the Lyrebird lacks in glamour,
it makes up in its vocal artistry.

2 November 2007

AUTUMN

A rising southerly
chases reluctant clouds
across a restless sky.
The warmth and brilliance of sunlight alternate
with the coolness and dullness
of a cloudy day.

Intermittently,
wind gusts in the trees,
the lonely call of a Currawong,
followed by sudden chirping of a late cricket.
In the distance,
the voice of laughing children.

After each wind burst,
the rustling of falling leaves
spiraling to earth, outside my window.
Rainbow coloured ones,
touched by a playful artist's palette,
others in many shades of brown.

Initially,
all green and tender,
holding the same promise.
Too soon,
some withered and died.
No sap, no life.

One last attempt by the sun rays
to pierce through the dense curtain of clouds.
Once more, the world comes alive
in a symphony of colours.
My room is bathed in light.
In one accord, the crickets start singing again.

As suddenly as it appeared,
the sunlight is gone.
The crickets stop.
Nature holds its breath.
Then, the sound of isolated raindrops.
Now, the steady drumming of rain.

6 April 1988

BUSY AS A BEE?

Seated at my usual breakfast spot,
in this place of rest and beauty,
looking out
at the flowering shrub
full of industrious bees,
I spot my favourite:
the round bumble bee!
Busy bees.

When I look again,
my bumble bee
is acting
somewhat out of sync.
Not so much interested
in flowers and their scent
but rather in leaves!?
Busy bee…?

Wholly focused on a leaf,
right in front of me;
is it exploring it?
Or maybe grooming itself?
Possibly suffering from stress?
Presently, it makes its way
underneath the leaf–
"Busy as a bee?"

That's where it attaches itself and,
after some wriggling,
remains perfectly still.
I finish my breakfast–
it's still there.
Then go about some mundane tasks-
and find it's still there.
Resting bee.

A brief conversation
takes my focus off the bee.
When I look again–
it is gone!
Showing
that even bees know
when it is time to stop!
Busy, yet wise as a bee!

Seaview Farm
St. Marys, Tasmania
17 February 2007

CELEBRATION OF LIGHT

Sunlight on water,
alternating with shade
from ancient trees.
Gentle ripples on the stream,
crowned by dancing sparkles,
laughing,
celebrating the light.

Sunrays,
piercing
this dark hiding place,
glittering
through my tears,
soothing
their unwelcome profusion.

7 February 2007
Goulburn River,
Seymour, Victoria

EVENING DANCE

A lingering sunset
at eventide.
The day seems to hold its breath
as the dusk gradually descends.
Not so the sea,
with its unceasing restlessness.

On the deserted beach,
near some houses,
a little girl absorbed in her sandy play.
Presently, a big dog sits down beside her.
"You are my friend", says the girl,
dancing around him.

Away they go,
running along the water's edge,
her little nightdress fluttering in the wind.
Then they sit and watch the mighty sea.
The world is theirs;
full of wonder for those with eyes to see.

"But everything is so big and
I am so little,"
the girl seems to think.
"Let's go back where we are safe!"
She takes the big dog by the collar
and pulls him back with force.

Unbeknown to both,
in the house nearest to them,
behind concealing curtains,
stand the watchful parents,
first laughing,
now their faces glowing.

Undated, possibly 1978
(re-written 2016)

FIREFLIES

Last night,
I went for a long walk
along the Daintree Forest,
on the road to Cow Bay.

I followed the bike trail,
meandering in and out
of the luscious rain forest,
and wished I had my bike.

Driven by inner pain,
I walked and walked.
An irrational desire
to beat the imminent dusk.

At "Crocodylus", I lingered long;
a series of large cabins,
picturesquely positioned
amidst the glorious rain forest.

Inside,
basic comfort.
See-through,
cool green mesh.

A direct link
to the surrounding majesty
of an ancient remnant-
nature at its best!

I should have headed back,
after that.
Instead,
I stubbornly kept walking.

Finally,
sense prevailed.
I turned back.
The sky a crimson afterglow.

Presently,
a stone bench and table
beckoned me,
near a disused "servo".

While pondering
the "For Sale" sign,
I thoroughly enjoyed
a strengthening snack.

I knew,
I wouldn't make it back
before the descending darkness
of the impending night.

Progressively,
the rain forest became dark
and mysterious,
as I finally made my way back.

Alternating
between bicycle lane
and main road,
I hastened my step.

The headlight of passing vehicles
briefly revealing
a lonely walker,
amidst the darkness.

Although now my pace was fast,
it wasn't driven by fear.
Rather, a sense of wonder
at the many noises near and far.

Suddenly,
my eye caught a spark.
It was a tiny, flickering dot,
moving to and fro.

Then, nearby,
at the edge of the rain forest,
a second one–
only those two.

I felt the same delight
of so many years ago when,
as a child, I would run after them–
fireflies!

I stood transfixed,
rewarded for lingering;
the dark forest revealing
one of its nocturnal wonders!

Cow Bay, Queensland
9 October 2006

GREY SUMMER'S DAY

Funny how,
when the sky clouds over,
things revive in the garden.
Especially near the storm water creek.
I hear the noisy, crashing sound
of a Lace Monitor passing through.
Imposing, prehistoric
seemingly slow and clumsy.
Yet, when with curiosity approached,
it heads for the nearest tree,
fast as lightening
and perfectly camouflaged!
Stay away sun,
just a little longer,
before your thirsty rays
dry up the creek once more
and shy monitor retreats deeper
into the bushland scrub!

5 February 2014

MERE WATCHING

Watching...
pen in hand, a cuppa by my side;
the water's playful ripple
driven by a gusty wind,
singing and rattling
around my little caravan.

Watching...
a silent pelican
calmly floating across the channel,
heading to its evening nesting ground.
With perfect grace and dignity,
it knows no haste nor tardiness.

Watching...
a continuous stream of cars
crossing the bridge to my right.
Opposite, the busyness of people-
shopping, working- doing.
Forgetting about the 'being'?

Watching...
the veiled yet blazing sunset-
a diva making her flamboyant exit,
surrounded by a spectacular entourage;
sombre, billowing clouds, gold edged,
on a background of vividly burnt orange.

Watching...
and exclaiming
a ridiculously inadequate "Wow!"
The silent lightening in the distance,
crowning this exuberant magnificence.
Humbled mankind- a mere spectator.

The Entrance North, New South Wales
24 October, 1999

MORE RAIN AHEAD

After many days of pouring rain,
the once lazy stagnant creek-
now a rushing powerful torrent,
filling the air with an unfamiliar sound,
like a distant highway full of semi-trailers,
or the approach of a mighty storm.
Closer to home-
the drip drop outside
from leaking gutters
and the random bell sounds
from chimes on the veranda,
stroked by capricious wind gusts.
Now, the rising and falling sound
of the last autumn crickets.

My ear strains to discern
between the sound of rain
and the wind in the trees.
A falling leaf, blowing against my window
stops short my autumn reverie.
The birds have ceased their song
and silent darkness has put the day to rest.
I close the shutters of my room,
straighten my sheets and pillows
then, slowly and aching, head for the kitchen.
The comfort of the whistling kettle.
I re-arm myself with more tissues and Panadol,
sighing as I hear the latest weather update:
more rain ahead!

5 March 1995

POETRY AGAIN

I am writing poetry again,
after all this time!
The chords struck
by a strange pain,
like a haunting melody,
evoked by a time and place.
Like the memory to the palate
of wine long in the making.
Similar, to a long forgotten,
familiar lingering fragrance
of an expensive perfume.
Or maybe,
like rediscovering
the glistening, colourful layers
forming the mighty rock,
brilliantly revealed after a storm.
Though not solid as rock,
rather,
elusive like morning mist,
dancing and rising in the valley,
soon making its exit.
Then,
returning again,
unexpectedly,
for a final encore.

29 April 1990

PREHISTORIC ERUPTION

A cataclysmic eruption of a
volcano, the size of a continent,
is covering a large part of the earth-
caustic dark ash
and noxious deadly fumes!

The sun, permanently eclipsed
by smoke clouds
blotting out the sky
and by rising poisonous gases,
swallowing up the whole world.

Now and then, the misty funeral shroud
torn open by an icy, arctic blast-
a sterile landscape is revealed.
The earth ash grey;
green breathed its last!

Black trees,
their naked limbs thrust upwards,
in dying desperation.
Nearby, the strewn, scarred remnants
of that colossi: dinosaur!

The curtains close once more.
Toxic fog takes over, darkness intensifies.
Apart from the howling storm,
no living thing moves.
Life has left for unknown millennia.

Undated, probably late 70's,
re-written 2016

SOUL BREATHING

Quiet houses on green hillsides.
Silent, gentle rain,
subdued cicadas
and occasional birds' twitter.
An intrusive car
soon fading in the distance.

Pale sunshine
on blades of grass.
Shiny leaves gently stirring.
Slow clouds wafting across the horizon,
torn asunder, then absorbing one another.
Grey changing to white.

Blue sky increases.
Sunlight returns
in full radiance.
The rain stops.
Resuming,
the piercing sound of cicadas.

I get up
and wonder
what to cook for dinner.

Ocean Shores, NSW
9 July 1985

SPRING MORNING

Newborn sun rays
casting long shadows across my path.
A cool breeze
swaying the gum tree hills.
Nearby, leaves gently rustling
and birds twittering.

As I cross the footbridge
over the railway line,
a crisp wind gust makes me shiver,
I pull my jacket tighter around me.
The highway below drowning out
Currawong, atop a tall Norfolk Pine.

I increase my pace
as I search for the silvery snake
in the distance.
Then I see it appear,
glistening in the morning sun.
On time!

I hurry to the end of the bridge,
trot along the highway strip,
up the stairs in a puff;
the attendant ready to blow the whistle.
Last step, then through the closing carriage door.
Phew! I just made it once again!

20 October 2003

THE BUMBLING BUMBLE BEE

Today, I chose a seat
at the long rustic table,
in the cottage's shared kitchen,
to have my breakfast.
I sat near the window,
overlooking the garden.

Outside, a lilac flowering plant
with long stems,
growing up past the window sill.
Mostly leaves, the flowers small,
in the shape of bells,
sun-drenched sparkling colours!

Bees, flying to and fro.
A round bumble bee,
selective in its choice of flowers,
joined the general busyness.
Its lovely shape and bright colours
filled my heart with merriment.

Aiming for the same flower,
a careless, smaller bee
made a last moment escape
from its larger counterpart.
Otherwise,
harmonious industriousness.

Suddenly, my tubby bumble bee
made an error of judgment;
it briefly attached to a flower
which could not hold its weight.
Both disappeared into the leafy undergrowth.
I laughed out loud at the jolly sight!

Then I watched anew
as the bee re-appeared,
resuming, red faced maybe?
its intensely focused labour.
No doubt,
with a little more care!

Seaview Farm, St. Marys, Tasmania
16 February 2007

THE PERFECTION OF SILENCE

Oh the bliss of wrapping myself in silence,
savouring time slowly, purposefully!
Allowing others to be,
whilst outside the ceaseless throng.

To watch birds,
riding wind currents
sculpting ripples on the water-
the ebb and flow of a tidal lagoon.

Noticing weather patterns
and their restless change.
No tecno infiltration.
No interruption to my train of thoughts.

Finally, to hum a tune,
feeling deep gratitude.
To savour, even just for a day,
the perfection of silence.

The Entrance North, New South Wales
24 October 1999

THE WALL OF STONES

I stayed in the bush,
on the Mountains called Blue.
The cottage,
touching on creative genius,
thoughtful to the needs of guests.

Love evident
for the medium used,
awakening awareness
of the unobtrusive beauty
of the Aussie bush.

Striking,
the attempt
to bring the bush inside.
Around the fireplace,
a wall built from local bush rocks.

In shape and colour,
not smooth and even
like bricks
but irregular and rustic-
each rock different.

While I breathed in the stillness,
the wall began to reveal
its coded message.
Differing rocks,
yet near-perfect symmetry.

Some functional,
while others jagged
(handle with care!).
Also, big and impressive,
while still others deep and 'holey'.

Once- sunning themselves or buried in the bush
(minding their own business).
Then- discovered, picked up and scrubbed clean.
Now- purposely positioned into a feature wall.
That speaks volumes to me! (1Pet. 2:4-5)

20 May 2003

Part 2

The Challenge of

RELATIONSHIPS

FOREWORD

*"Success is not final,
failure is not fatal:
it is the courage to continue
that counts."*

Winston Churchill

Some of us came into this world and continue living with a definite deficit in the area of love. We were either considered an inconvenience from the outset, too high a price to pay for someone's precious independence or else parented by parents who also had suffered from the same syndrome and therefore handicapped in the capacity to nurture and care for a little human, with huge, scary needs.

Such were my early beginnings and by the time I became a teenager, I battled with many "demons". Depression was one of them. My saving grace was the resolute determination that I wasn't going to spend the rest of my life staying emotionally handicapped.

Life inexorably moved forward and demanded decisions from me; decisions I had no real understanding about, except what the movie screen presented at that time, and to some extent still does. The stark reality though, presented on our screens these days regarding relationships, must seem even more confusing for those at the start of their adult lives!

One of the quotes from my poem "The Diary" sums up my life experience up to then: "experiences of pseudo-love and destructive love games. The fake is recognized only by knowing the real first."

Only since I have come to experience and learn about God's love for me in Christ and seen the reality of my consequent changed life, in every area, do I finally know what real love looks like. It is of course the purest love there is which, as Christians we are encouraged to follow and to show to the world. It requires putting self-centered needs second. It is amazing how life-giving, to others and to self, such practice, energized by His Spirit, really is!

I have not tried to hide how broken and self-absorbed I have been at times and still can be. It is part of my desire to reveal myself to my readers, warts and all! "We have this treasure in earthen vessels" we read in the Scriptures (2 Cor. 4:7). It is in our brokenness that we can identify with one another, yet we are called to become "like Him" (1 John 3:2) and that "He who has started a good work in you will complete it..." (Phil. 1:6).

My emotional life used to be like a roller coaster. Through an unceasing search after wholeness, by God's grace and much help and prayer from His people and those He put into my path, I have found ongoing peace and real, lasting joy!

I therefore thank first my God and Saviour for the gift of salvation, which is a privilege that has many layers to it, and every precious person whom God has used to bring greater insight and healing to me. I am forever indebted to you all! THANK YOU.

P.H.-G.

A PRISTINE DAY

Standing inside the beautiful inlet,
surrounded by shallow water,
not a soul around but us two,
you with your fishing rod.
The day is pristine,
a soft wind in the trees
A picture of perfection
except inside of us!

We've had another quarrel-
the second in a row.
Tempers frayed anew.
You, getting very bossy.
I, perplexed, incredulous,
then very, very blue.
It always seems to happen
when we're away together, on holidays!

My anger dissipated,
my stubborn will all but crushed.
I turn my back to you and battle tears,
conscious of this silent pathos,
reinforced by a sense of déjà vu.
What had promised to be paradise,
has turned into a prison of pain and fear.
And still more layers surfacing!

A legacy of distrust and pain, impotence and rage
which, back then, I medicated with a vow:
"No one would ever boss me again!"
Then I go and marry you;
at times, kind and caring
but also very controlling!
Suddenly, you're putting your arm around me…
Finally we listen and talk!

> Cuttagee Lake, New South
> Wales, April 2004

A SERIES OF BRIEF ENCOUNTERS

Out of the blue,
you came for a single visit.
You slept in the other bed,
in the guestroom of your father-in-law's pub.
That room was my nursery;
for lack of guests staying over.
My trunk in the corner,
inside all my toys and things,
quickly put out of sight, if need be-
a multi-functional set-up.
A little child in a large bed, in a big room.
We played a simple game of pop the cheeks,
resulting in peals of giggles and laughter.
I thought you finally loved me…

At seventeen, I had a dream.
With some help,
I managed to track you down.
A meeting ensued;
I tried so hard
to be pleasant, funny, pretty,
like going for an interview.
Your interest lasted a whole week.
Then, the all too familiar silence.
No answer to my letters.
No response to my wedding invitation.
I let go.
I stopped trying.
Stopped crying.

In my thirties,
with two young children,
newly divorced,
I happened to be in your area
(in your part of the globe).
I was told that you were very ill.
A meeting was arranged by someone.
I could find no pity when we met,
nor could I show a smile.
Just silent coldness.
The little child, now woman
had closed her door,
her once hopeful heart
had turned to ice.

The last meeting between us
was in a dream.
You approached me.
Your pleading eyes
asked for forgiveness
for the indifference
the neglect,
the failure of a father
to acknowledge his daughter.
I just turned away –
the door had been closed to you
a very long time ago!
Much later, I heard that, around that time,
you had passed away.

That dream haunted me
throughout the years.
Gradually,
the ice began melting.
A new sorrow
began emerging.
I finally realized that,
of all evil,
unforgiveness is the greatest one.
For if my loving Heavenly Father
could and does forgive me,
why not also forgive
my earthly father's failure
to show love to me?

30 March 2001

AN UNSURRENDERED HEART

It's a tug of war,
a fight for the dubious privilege
to sit on the throne of my heart.
Memories flashing past,
arousing,
caressing,
tempting.
Your face,
your hands,
even the way you walk
and the sweetness of the taste
of the forbidden fruit.
"Seek the things that are above".
Yet,
I revel in the soft autumn breeze,
the warm sunlight upon my face,
the rustling of the trees,
the white downy clouds
rushing across a cobalt sky,
the verdant fields and woods around me
and the memory of your love-
and the anticipated gamble
of its working out.

27 March 1984

AND I THOUGHT WE WERE FRIENDS!

After a night of too much food,
Champagne and "Krambambuli",
of seeming merriment
and quadruple fireworks displays,
I sit at my desk,
my heart tight
inside my chest.

We have spent a lifetime,
so it seems,
discussing our differing views.
For a long time,
they seemed to me
well humoured discussions,
though not lacking in conviction.

Lately though,
you have been throwing
fiery daggers of enmity
which I, unawares,
now incredulous
have allowed
to my very core.

Are you seeing me differently?
Or maybe only now
showing your true colours?
I have found it hard to believe
the seeming depth of your venom.
You always used to show courtesy-
contempt finally corroding that veneer.

Are we presently condemned
to relate in shallow merriment?
To dance around each other
in weary, cautious moves?
Or is this a long-overdue awakening
of a fact I tended to embellish?
That there never was substance from the start!

1 January 2005

AWAKENING

Again,
I had this wish
you might find me
and take me away,
to a life of awakening.

My feelings,
no longer asleep,
rather,
breaking forth
to escape this spell.

Your presence,
to me like the prince's kiss
for the timid Cinderella.
Springtime's scents and sights
finally restored to me.

The world,
now small and restricted,
opened up for us to be discovered.
You would even delay
the ebbing away of my youth.

In the end,
I waited in vain;
you are not seeking after me.
I heard you found someone else.
A new awakening put on hold once again.

Undated

(Probably late 1970's)

CARS PASSING

Drumming rain,
and the ebb and flow of cars passing.
Lying in the dark, waiting.

Your tears could not touch me.
Indifferent shame?
Why then these tears?
Nothing really matters.
It's all the same to me.
Tears and laughter.
Passion and indifference.
Day and night.
They all meet somewhere.
Now, I allow both to come.
Sometimes though, I forget.

The rain has ceased.
Only the sound of passing cars.
Lying in the dark, waiting.

November 1980

CAT AND MOUSE GAME

For so long,
I have sensed your pull
but put it down to mere attraction.

I have become tired
of playing games;
mere superficial outputs of the heart.

Yet,
that certain undefinable something
has remained.

Responding to you with coolness,
at times indifference;
finding myself on the receiving end of the same.

You have noticed me
foolishly giving my heart away,
only to receive it back bruised.

I can see,
we have been watching one another;
who's the cat and who's the mouse here?

My stance: detachment and slight irony.
Yours: uncanny and unnerving certainty,
or so it seems to me!

My view on this has changed now;
irony muted into uneasiness,
tinged with fear.

Worse still,
to my bewilderment and surprise-
I now am longing for your love and care!

My fear is that, as soon as you find out,
this victory might be all you were waiting for,
in order to turn your back on me!

9 August 1985

COCKROACHES

The room is like a cell.
Naked, white walls.
A bare bulb dangling,
shedding a cold, glaring light.
Black, shiny insects crawling around me.
Hundreds of cockroaches
swarming near me,
barely finding space.
Climbing over each other,
Then over my feet.

They fly against the walls,
dropping heavily to the ground.
A buzzing sea,
trying to engulf me.
Never ending chaos,
resonating within me.
Should I counter this creeping
with an act of desperate fury?
Not stopping,
till all have been crushed?

Now,
a door opens;
a call to quickly leave!
I brush off a few of the insects,
vigorously shake my head
and move my fingers through my hair.
Then run for the exit.
One last glance,
The door slams shut behind me.
I awake with a start.

Undated
(Probably around mid-1970's)

EMPTY

Sitting in the car,
waiting.
Empty.
All day talking-
untouched.
Laughter shared,
yet alone.
Game playing,
draining.
Discomfort,
best pushed away.
Complex pieces,
not fitting.
Longing
for harmony,
depth,
patterns matching,
colours blending,
truly relating,
connecting.
In vain.

28 July 1987

FAILED HARVEST

So much promise in that fruit!
Within it-
all the intensity
of a potential rich harvest.
Eagerly awaiting
the early rains,
the sun's warmth
and the earth's sustenance.

The rains were not due yet.
The sun's rays but weak
and the earth-
in its wintery sleep.
Bravely,
it persevered
with so much hope
and faith.

How long?
At some unknown point,
the point of no return,
that eager life within
started to let go.
Flickering, and gradually fading,
till it went out-
dropping to the ground.

That fruit was my undeclared love for you.
A love that nearly drove me to despair.
We were young then, too young.
Just when I could see a glimmer of hope-
life tore us apart.
Aging now and alone,
I mourn for that lost hope
of an early autumn harvest.

29 October 2012

FEELING RAW

Feeling raw,
as if coarse sandpaper
had been chafing my insides,
tearing up old wounds.

Expressing my pain
further worsens it
by your indignant denial,
adding disappointment to the mix.

Am I expected
to accept tokenistic caring?
Overt patronizing
and public humiliations?

I must rightly read what's there,
and see why I chose as I did.
Also, realize that no one deserves
to be treated such – no one!

Once fully accepted-
to take appropriate action,
whatever this action might be.
All I know: I deserve better!

I deserve better, **now**.
Not tomorrow, nor in the by and by.
Knowing this, will bring its own answer.
I don't fear what it may be.

10 October 2002

FOOL'S GOLD?

Some say,
"See how ugly he can be?
How much meanness,
even baseness is in him?
A coward,
and you know it!".
"Yes", she says.
"All this seems to be part of him,
I am aware of it.
Yet,
lately,
I have looked into a small window
of his heart,
usually kept tightly barricaded.
There,
I found kindness,
even a touch of beauty.
That's where I will put my hope.
I have witnessed his longing
for that hidden man within.
Only love can lead him to himself."
Like digging for gold-
some spend their all on fool's gold.
Some will persevere and find the real thing.

19 October 1978

FRAGMENTS

With a furious sword,
life has dashed to pieces
the core of his being.
Fragments are all that's left of him.

In a vain attempt at wholeness,
he seeks to find it in the fragment,
never knowing who he is.
Cynicism masking his brokenness.

His spirit asleep,
he is driven
by shifting sands,
rigidly adhering to external stability.

Could he but for a moment
look away from himself
and his unceasing quest,
a surprising thing may happen.

He could then see
that the very brokenness,
which fills him with hidden shame,
if embraced and surrendered, could bring life.

Weakness would be exchanged
for strength.
Ashes of grief and loss,
for the joy of new beginnings.

Simply, by laying down,
once and for all,
the old torn self
at the foot of the cross.

12 January 1993

FRIENDS

True and tried friends:
like shady trees,
on a hot summer's day.
Colourful flowers,
amongst rock and gravel.
A sweet drink with lots of ice,
after a long and weary walk.
Shiny ribbons and wrappings
around presents
under the Christmas tree.
Like waking up to a clear and sweet melody,
on a cool morning, in early Spring.
Or a dive in the pool,
after a hot and sticky day.
Even like a richly laid out banqueting table
you spot when first arriving at a dinner party.
In short, friends are the sugar and the spice
that make your life tasty, sweet and nice!

6 January 1987

FUTURE RESPONSE

No matter how endearing I may try to be-
I cannot control your future response!
For all I know and there is to see:
you're presenting your best side to me.

Once yours, will you turn from your kindness?
Anxious questions arise.
Drop your guard and reveal my blindness?
Disappointment to rob me of soundness?

Those smiling blue eyes in which I bask,
can they reveal if your love is real?
Can your poetry or your kisses, I ask?
And can you guarantee it will last?

I can decide to be true,
as I cannot guarantee your future response.
To continue to love and not be blue,
should loving response diminish from you.

31 November 1994

I KNOW

(Describing a relationship
I was watching close up)

Every time you leave me,
I die.

Though my death is not peace,
more like hell.
It is hopeless hope.

Then you come back-
and everything seems unreal:
my hell a mere illusion.
I don't understand it anymore.

Your presence–
a heavenly torture!
I know I have lost you.
I know what you feel
when you look at me that way.

I cling to you,
when you try to free yourself.
I try to charm you,
fully knowing
and reading in your eyes
that I have lost all charms.

I know how foolish,
to try to please you
when you are pushing me away.
I laugh, though I feel like crying.
It would only shorten your presence.
When you are gone, I will be free.
Then, my death will be complete.

London
February 1968

IMPROMPTU PERFORMANCE

On the sidewalk sits a lonely figure,
creating strange sounds
with his age old instrument.
Rapt in a trance,
strumming his chords,
while indifferent people rush past.
A group of adolescents
amuse themselves on nearby steps,
throwing coins into the musician's basket.
Grubby children stand around watching,
curiosity in their eyes.
The musician continues to play,
nodding when a coin is thrown.
His eyes gaze into nowhere.
A group of people stop and watch.
One of them slowly pulls out a flute
and continues to listen.
Then he brings it to his lips
and tentatively joins in.
Slowly unfolding between them,
a melody.
It steadily gains in liveliness,
until both instruments
merge into perfect harmony.
People stand still,
look puzzled,
then smile,
rocking to the music.

Byron Bay, New South Wales
undated (80's)

JUST A DREAM

Last night,
I dreamt of you.
This morning,
again,
this strange consuming fire.
Do not worry my heart,
there is no fuel
to keep the fire burning.
You remain
unattainable as ever.
Soon,
those flames-
mere embers
and finally,
cold ash.
Once again,
the grey returns,
with its dull comfort.

Written in 1981

JUST FOR YOU

Have you ever felt
a feather-light breeze,
gently stirring your face?
Does a falling leaf,
at times,
lightly graze your cheek,
before it settles on the ground?
When you stretch out,
to absorb the last rays of a setting sun,
do you feel gentle warmth upon your skin?
And when snow falls,
do the dancing snowflakes
softly caress your face and hair?
It is my hand that's stretching out to you
and my fingers that softly stroke your skin.

Written in 1979

LIVING WITH UNEASINESS

What is this feeling in my pit?
This wrenching in my gut?
Like a knife turning.
Playing the blame game.
I catch that ball.
It weighs a ton!
Why catch it in the first place?

Like trying to lift a load,
too smooth to tackle.
Or turning a heavy mattress,
with no handles to hold.
Mountains,
or mole hills?
Merely an overactive mind?

Lying awake,
one more night.
In vain,
waiting for sleep to return.
I finally grab that little white pill.
It does for me
what I can't do for myself.

11 December 2007

LONGING

Alone in a hotel room,
he craves for her, convinced
that the immensity of his hunger
could not ever be satisfied.

Lying near her now,
he envisages a walk,
alone,
on a deserted beach.

Weary from yet another childbirth,
her hair in her eyes,
she gazes out into cold and stark whiteness,
her sick child finally asleep.

Hunched on a park bench,
the old spinster looks at the little child,
absorbed in a coloured leaf,
and forgets to throw bread to the pigeons.

Secretly,
the girl looks at the kissing lovers,
entwined in a primal embrace
and cannot fall asleep at night.

Her hands over her bulging body,
the young woman, longingly,
looks at the laughing schoolgirls,
passing near her window.

September 1978

LOST DREAMS

They robbed her of her dream
and smashed it in a hundred pieces.
For comfort, they made her believe
that it was a fake
of the real thing.

She used to find refuge in that dream.
Now she doesn't know
where to start looking for it.
Unexpectedly,
she finds one of the shattered pieces.

The rest have been dispersed
by a mocking wind,
irreparably so.
They have lost their dreams,
why shouldn't she?

Undated
Probably late 70's or early 80's

MAKING A STAND

Blank.
Flat.
Sitting alone
in a café,
after a futile confrontation.
We both agreed,
(not agreeably)
to disagree.

Two incidents,
involving
two (or too) differing people.
Two scenarios,
two attempts
at trying to shake
that
which cannot be shaken.

Should I feel bad
that some things
cannot be moved?
Why can't you accept
that sometimes,
I need to make a stand?
A stand is a stand.
Not a shuffle.

Could it be that those
who don't want to make a stand,
resent mostly those
who can and do?
Today, I slammed the door
on half-hearted apologies,
on past & present berating and
on a litany of expectations.

30 March 2001

NO ONE TOLD ME BACK THEN

No one told me
what I should have been told
about love.
Natural attraction
should not be the determining factor
to make a final choice.
Life-long commitment
requires loyalty, selflessness
and endurance, in order to last.
I needed to be careful,
in order not to sell myself short
and not miss the very best.

To guard my heart,
the most precious thing
about myself.
The state of my heart
dictating the quality of my life.
Instead, these memories-
a mixture of bitter sweet.
More bitter, than sweet.
I could have been spared
much heartache and tears.
But then again...
no one really understood back then!

5 October 2012

ODE TO A SOUL-MATE DREAM

While away,
with much time on my hands
to think and write,
I find myself re-reading
ancient love letters of mine to you,
given back to me;
an encounter with a young self.

Between the lines,
a persistent theme,
a thread,
repeatedly leading me astray.
A dream,
which has followed me
all my life.

A sweet foretaste
of that which didn't come to pass;
to find and deeply love
that much anticipated soul-mate.
Instead,
I hold these letters of dreams,
returned to me- they didn't seem to fit.

My mother,
who hardly knew me,
nor made the time,
called me
"nothing but a dreamer".
Dreams
without substance?

If she knew,
she didn't show me
how to manage dreams.
Unknowingly,
could she have been
pouring contempt
on her own broken dreams?

As for me,
those dreams were mine alone,
my own responsibility.
Foolishly,
I tried to make them yours as well.
Lacking the insight
that they needed to fit us both!

Did I believe then
that love alone
would surely put it right?
Remove all obstacles?
Was I saturated
by dangerous lies,
presented to us on the movie screen?

What I found instead
was that love
is needed mainly
to bring release.
Professions of undying love,
couldn't even stop the insult
of the wandering eye.

Strange,
how two separate honeymoons
like omens,
were spent with husbands,
both on sickbeds.
Walking in honeymoon gardens,
alone.

Today,
I heard the call
to put that broken dream
finally to rest.
It felt like a part of me
being ripped out
of my heart.

The hope
of finding fulfilment
of that long-held desire,
and the anticipation of ensuing sweetness-
for both of us.
Almost unbearable,
to part with that life-long dream!

Even now, that I am aging,
it will not willingly go.
Except for that call
to a new and higher dream,
which must stand alone.
Demanding
all others to be put to death.

This dream-
A King's dream
for His beloved Bride.
His call-
Arise, to taste of His love
and to let Him lead,
despite the dying involved.

I will wait for Him,
and seek Him
with new hope in my heart.
"Winter is past",
He says,
"the rains are over and gone".
Spring is here.
(Song of Songs 2:11-13).

Culburra Beach, New South Wales
12 October 2012

PAIN

All through the night,
I listen to the struggled breathing
of my feverish child.
When I call your name,
there is no answer.
I go near your bed-
greyness
the expression of your face.
Empty and withering,
I want to release
these choking feelings,
without being able
to shed one single tear.
Most painful of all:
feeling
and being made to feel
that the cause of all this,
lies inside
my very own self!

Undated, 1978 approx.

PLAYING WITH FIRE

The dreams she can read in his eyes
no longer are about her.
The silence between them
doesn't speak of togetherness.
The love songs they listen to
won't draw them together.
Even the full moon he contemplates
takes him far from her.
Everything that brought him close to her,
now pushes him away further.

I can see all this;
that I am pulling him away from her.
Playing with fire-
of a dangerous kind.
I know full well, right from wrong.
This belongs to the latter.
Yet I cannot
will not,
cease searching for his eyes
and bathe in the warmth they radiate.

(Undated, probably 1984 or earlier)

PREDATOR

We talked about love.
A surprise visitor;
a friend of friends
and I, his host,
giving him a lift
to the station.
I talked about Agape-
the most powerful force
in all the universe!
He just laughed.
I could detect
embarrassment
in his laughter.

My friends failed to disclose:
Passion,
this he knew.
Obsession,
his daily bread.
Perversion,
a preferred trademark.
In typical predatory style,
well known to his kind,
I later realized-
he had tried to proposition
my beautiful twelve-year old
to go with him to a distant land!

30 March 1988

QUITTING

You think you've got reasons
to quit.
"Always a looser",
you state.
"Tried,
for a long time now-
No go!"
That makes two of us.
"Some never get a fair go",
you say.
"Crippled",
you call it,
"before we could walk".
What's new?
You put the blame
on your world.
"Dog eats doggy",
and so on.
You feel like
crawling into a hole
and falling asleep,
for a very long time.
So do I.
Then again-
the only losers
are quitters!

31 July 1987

RED CARNATIONS

(Dedicated to Betty Carver)

Your garden's red carnations
exude a perfume from long ago.
They evoke childhood memories,
when flowers were uniquely different;
not just by looks but also by scent.

Old fashioned red carnations-
simple, unobtrusive.
Not like the showy roses,
nor the exotic profusion of orchids.
They are happy to bloom in everyday gardens.

These red carnations,
unlike jasmine and wisteria,
whose perfume is heady and pervasive;
their scent is appreciated only
by those who would draw near.

Your gift of red carnations,
a token to gladden my heart and soul,
have a sweetness that is constant.
They are a perfect expression
of your friendship and love.

16 December 2002

SECRET GARDEN

Come with me
to a grand tour
of my secret garden.

I give you the key
to the old iron gate,
inside the wall.

The perfume of honeysuckle,
overhanging the wall,
permeates the air.

You may bring
a jar of your tears
and whispers of your heart.

Leave such weights as fear-
shadows of the night,
at the foot of the gate.

As you wander through the garden,
I will be there beside you
discovering anew its secrets.

Water abounds in my garden.
It lies sleepily in quiet ponds
and sings merrily in winding brooks.

At times, they turn into raging torrents,
which could sweep you away,
together with leaves and branches.

Deep within the center of the garden,
dark and jagged crevices loom.
Remnants of past tremors and devastation.

I'll lead you safely around those.
Just hold my hand;
we will need to tread softly there.

My garden isn't all sweet and serene.
Intruders will find it treacherous,
whereas you are my welcome guest.

December 1994

SIMPLY THANK YOU

Dear one,
I want to thank you,
while the clouds,
like the curtain on a stage,
have been pulled back,
allowing the sun-rays to break through.
Thank you for taking me
to see the thundering sea,
the towering peaks
and the glens of ferns,
gently quivering in the misty rain.
Thank you for showing me
the rare and solitary orchid,
hidden amongst rocks
and thorny shrubs.
For the laughter,
the cups of coffee,
sitting on windy hillsides,
overlooking a sea of trees,
or crashing waves.
For your letters,
tenderly describing
the sky,
Fish River,
and creatures,
appearing unexpectedly.
For those poet's words of yours,
causing my rusty heart strings
to reverberate to the tune
of a symphony in the making.

Thank you for holding on,
through those howling storms,
which put Tracey to shame.
For your cupped hands
around the wildly flickering flame.
Thank you.

28.12.1995

SUBSTITUTES

Grasping
for glitter.
A brief struggle to get;
when finally won,
the interest is gone.

Not daring
to believe
for that which really satisfies.
Instead, elbowing
for short-lived substitutes.

Undated
Possibly written in 1980's

TENTS DANCING

Hot, dry wind
over parched desert land,
swirling up sand,
stinging eyes and partly exposed faces-
mainly of women and children,
queuing for their daily rations.
A sea of tents,
as far as the eye can see.
Makeshift homes for refugees;
once large families
with a desire to prosper,
to give a future to their offspring.
Also, to offer shelter
to their aging parents,
and to enjoy status
in their communities.
War tore them asunder;
killing, raping and maiming,
indiscriminately.
Presently,
reduced to the status of beggars.
A perceived burden.
A political football.
Stateless
and homeless.
Their dignity left behind.
After the numbness of grief,
what is there left
but blame?
Easy targets
for ideologies of hatred.

Usually,
towards "meddlers from the West"!
They came with guns and tanks
and a self-righteous demeanour.
They are usually the ones
now offering charity,
expecting gratitude.
Why not bite the hand,
perceived to have held a gun?
When hatred prevails,
truth becomes irrelevant.
Whose truth, anyway?
The war may have been left behind
but is now raging
in wounded human hearts.
As quick as it arose
the wind has died down.
The shimmering heat
causing tents to dance,
on waves of scorching sand.

29 September 2013

THE ALLY

After yet another night of tossing,
the revelation
that I have lost my ally,
since losing your favour.

I have concluded
that it is too costly
trying to humour you
on a continuous basis.

"What kind of ally?"
I asked myself.
"Why should I need an ally?"
Questions not asked before.

Have I been living
with a warped raison d'être?
Some phobic angst maybe,
about "them and us"?

My unannounced appearance-
an unwanted 'baby bump',
forced my parents to take a step
which eventually undid us all.

Every which way,
both turned away from me.
Gone were what should have been
my greatest allies.

Other carers too busy
with their own lives.
Fickle allies, to be sure.
Allies and accusers, all in one.

The more allies then,
the more chance
to keep the pointing at bay?
You seem to practice this belief.

By not humouring your outlook,
I end up in opposition.
Expressions of our hidden fears
towards one another.

This warped perception
and warlike inner stance
only thrives in the darkness
of our hidden primeval fears.

Presently, as for me,
I have two allies only
against ignorance
and inner and outer lies.

God, who died for me
and I,
who made a pact with self:
always "to thine own self be true"!

Undated, possibly December 1998

THE APPENDIX

The lie
of their perception
and of the gradual becoming
a mere appendix.
An extension of someone else.

Trying to connect,
only to realize;
all I shall ever be
in their eyes-
just an appendix.

A part of the real thing,
of the desired one,
of the one that matters.
The inner circle will only connect
with their own kind.

I see it
and then I don't.
The inner ache reminds me;
there cannot be connection
when you're on the outer.

To simply love is not enough;
mere tolerance- all you get in return.
To want to be loved by all
is naïve in the extreme,
a recipe for pain.

Looking in all the wrong places,
that foolish little child
is led astray by a smile.
Driven by blind hunger
to belong and to be loved.

Why then stay where hunger
only gets crumbs?
Why dwell at the edge of starvation
where the disguised face of lack
exalts the meagre fare?

Instead of searching
for that which sustains,
it seems easier
to just…
keep barely alive.

A clever ploy or diabolical scheme
in order to keep one in fetters
while feeding them lies?
Weaving gossamer blankets
that cannot give warmth.

Trying to convince
that the hunger
is really satiation.
The cold merely the result
of a distorted reality.

18 October 2003

THE BIRTH

Part of our training-
witnessing my first birth!
Painfully aware of cold white walls,
glaring lights over a writhing woman's body,
held and surrounded by those in charge.

An oppressive picture
of crushing humiliation;
bloodstained sheets
and agonized screams-
I turn my head away.

A wave of excitement now.
The peak of expectation can be felt.
Raised voices from the staff
giving instructions to the mother.
Rapidly increasing, a dark mass emerging.

A small head,
growing into shoulders,
chest and arms,
and soon
into a slimy, slippery human being.

"The matching outcome
of this labour of ugliness",
my ignorant self concludes.
Soon the room is filled
with a loud and miserable sound.

I shiver at the coldness around me.
All I want is for this to be over.
Then I look at the mother
stretching out her hands,
holding the noisy bundle against her.

I cannot take my eyes off her face.
All agony vanished from it.
Instead
there is a light,
a smile so gentle.

Her hands stroking the baby,
seem strong and warm.
Again, I turn away my head;
to hide the tears
that secretly roll down my face.

July 1979

THE DIARY

> Dedicated to Roland

Seeing life's autumn creep up on me,
the need arose
to finally bring closure
to an old flame of mine.

The impetus–
an old re-surfaced diary
which opened up a Pandora's Box,
filled with longing and pain.

Anew, it knocked me off my feet!
Why this intensity?
Who was this boy,
evoking such uncaused pain?

Why could I never speak to him?
A search commenced
to finally get some answers.
And lo! A response!

Back then, I should have known
and now discovered:
Like Dante and Beatrice,
my existence- unknown to him!

Worse than Tillandsia,
I had fed on airy hopes
and future projection:
distorted images of love.

Then, the sum-total
of life's primary relationships.
Throughout early life-
abuse, neglect and abandonment.

Lately, bullying and ridicule,
my daily diet.
Fear of rejection,
my safe hiding place.

People had been cruel;
my image of him- Christ-like.
A bubble that wouldn't burst,
if not touched.

Fifty years later,
the bubble finally burst;
a strange, liberating emptiness lingering.
An after-taste of death.

Death, made up of past toxic pain,
wrong beliefs
and distorted, illusionary thinking
about love.

Later, experiences of pseudo-love
and destructive love games.
The fake is recognized only
by knowing the real first.

Now, all safely nailed to the cross. Not
mysterious religion
but life-giving reality,
being in Christ, through faith.

Not returning to fantasy and make-believe
but touched by the Real.
Continuously receiving life-changing,
life-enhancing and life-supporting grace.

I put the lock back on my diary,
the lid on the empty Pandora's Box
and added one more chapter
to the story of my life.

6 March 2013

THE GUARDIAN

Today
I said adieu
to my old guardian.
A legacy of my childhood
I had been clinging to
for far too long.
He served me well,
keeping those bullies at bay,
teasing and taunting me,
waiting for me in alleyways
during my school years.
The timid victim,
after reading
a certain book,
turned into a war machine,
driven by indignant rage,
showing them what they were:
mere cowards at best!

I now realize
this build-up of anger,
once unleashed
causes untold damage
to self and others.
There are better ways
to deal with
seeming wrongs.
Anger felt
needs to be acknowledged.
Anger expressed,
carefully filtered.

The instinctive response
replaced
with a God-inspired
and adult one.
Time to grow up
a little bit more.

The Old Covenant of law
has been fulfilled
by the new covenant of grace.
The time has come
to bravely let go of the old
and entrust myself
to the Safe Keeper
of faith and trust.
Injuries
keep turning up.
Insults
make their way to my door.
It happens to all.
How to continue to respond?
My default mode
isn't the way of life in Him now.
His life
must and will come forth!

28 January 2008

THE IDOL

"Trust me," he said.
I tried, in vain.
He didn't measure up.
Didn't conform.
Didn't fit the mould.
The pattern of the image which,
long ago,
I put my trust in.
When realized,
it would fulfil all my hopes.
Releasing the woman within.
The hoped for cast of man,
w
h
i
c
h

n
o
w

h
a
d

b
e
c
o
m
e
mere idolatry.

5 August 1996

THE MASQUERADE

I went to a masquerade,
where everyone followed the rules-
except me.

All busy acting their part,
happy and with abandon-
except me.

"How ridiculous their disguise", I thought.
"They are only fooling themselves-
except me."

"I will resist and show conviction.
Some might take off the mask they're wearing-
except me."

Then one of them, with amused expression,
with a sweeping gesture
bowed very low in front of me.

"Your courage is admirable".
"No doubt, I would follow your example,
but for one thing:

You lack gaiety, nor feel at ease.
You might convince someone else-
except me!"

20 February 1976

THE ROAD TO FREEDOM

Unkindness and evil abound,
leaving torment and misery
in their wake,
making life a burden.
The soft heart of a child changed
into the stony heart of mankind.

The word you used was "scum".
"None worth a crumpet,
treacherous at every turn,
the more of them you get to know!"
An expert at protective self-deception,
you simply don't trust anyone!

Attracted to the ones in kind,
you feel to be the wise one,
having figured it all out,
boasting of outsmarting "them".
Laughing at those foolish ones, talking of love.
"Airheads!" Yet their serenity unnerves you.

Hard, cunning, yet straining at the reel.
Feeling disliked and deeply lonely.
"Ah, what rubbish!" you say.
"Just a touch of lingering sentimentality,
probably instilled by mushy aunts at babyhood."
And, "We are men and men are made of steel!"

Your sons, while little, had many fears.
They were too soft, you said.
They needed toughening up.
You mocked them for their frailty.
Softness would not survive in this harsh world.
They hid in shame and cried bitter tears.

Not only did they hide from softness –
they also hid from you!
You counted on them becoming like you
but got a simmering hatred instead.
They had become hard alright!
Directed at you was their loathing.

Loneliness grasped you with its iron clasp.
Self-doubt found your Achilles heel.
Sudden bursts of rage,
in-between dark brooding.
Lingering over drink,
your bitterness an ever deepening cesspool.

Finally, you had to admit:
"Where did I go wrong?"
The pain you felt was the pain of death,
which has a way of breaking us,
if we cannot bend with it.
Wisdom waiting to bring life out of ashes.

"Still Waters", Budgewoi
8 February 2005

THE TOXIC PARENT

How can seeming kindness
be so toxic?
Is it that it has more to do
with the giver,
than with the one given to?
The charity syndrome,
which enhances the giver,
at the expense of the receiver?
An unspoken "you should be grateful!"
ringing in my ears.
With all that giving,
I become the poorer,
more disempowered.
Feeling less capable
and more inadequate.
Maybe, it is to do
with your unceasing attempt
to teach me
your so-called better ways.
The trouble is-
I feel so undervalued.
Handicapped
in your eyes.
One such remark
triggers a thousand memories.

I gaze into mirrors,
of mirrors,
of mirrors,
down the hallway of time.
To you,
I still seem
the untimely fruit
of your body.
The embarrassment
of your past.
The blemish,
that won't go away.
Is that why
you cannot let me be me?

Zurich, Switzerland
15 October 2005

TIME

Already,
time is eroding
the memory
of you.

Your presence,
once an inseparable part of me,
now moving away
from me.

The once piercing pain
tearing at my heart,
becoming dull
with the passing of time.

Your image,
just recently
sharp and strong,
becoming blurred.

Straining
to remember
the traits
of your face.

Where there was trust,
more and more doubts arising.
"We need to grow, separately,
each one in our own way."

This is what you
said. I only hope we
won't grow apart.

Undated
Probably late 1970's

TO WRITE POETRY

Surrounded by dusty furniture,
fresh washing to be folded,
dry and droopy flowers in a vase,
and dirty dishes in the sink–
the urge to write poetry!

Despite insistent cries from hungry cats,
circling and rubbing around my legs,
the guilt of unanswered letters,
and bills spilling out everywhere-
the irresistible pull to write poetry!

Despite uncertainty,
as to worth and skill
of my unpolished art,
playful and untamable-
the choice to write poetry!

5 March 1995

TOUCHED BY THE DIVINE

(A Prophetic Poem)

A shy young woman's unrequited love.
Sighing and tears unending,
falling on barren ground.
Later, tossed and twisted
by life's chaotic events.

A whirlwind of demands,
gradually
spiraling downward.
Greying hair,
slowing step.

Finally,
pen in hand,
processing those events.
The memory of that distant love,
re-awakening pain and grief.

Daring now
and curious.
Did he ever know?
Locating him –
easier than she thought.

A surprised but open response.
From a distance
she finally finds out
that he never knew her,
nor of her love back then.

In a poem to him
she shares
about her love now,
for the One
Who loves them both.

The One
whose picture
was marred for him
by religion back then,
when she loved him.

Her plea to him now:
'Dare to look beyond
that false portrait'.
This encounter
deeply touches him.

Gradually,
his initial reluctance ebbing away.
In its stead,
uncovering a hidden treasure,
filling a void that had always been there.

By an act of divine grace,
those seemingly wasted tears,
anointed by the Divine
become rivers of life that now bring eternity
to a soul otherwise forever lost.

6 July 2014

(Vision given by revelation,
believed in faith)

"Nearly all of God's jewels are crystallized tears."
Anon

TRANSITION

She is looking for freedom
but to the first lover
she gives away her heart.
She wants to expand,
to reach out.
Then, at the first cold wind,
she runs for shelter.
She says she never feels lonely,
why then is she waiting so anxiously
for his step to approach?
She says it doesn't matter if he won't come.
That she will laugh at her own crazy dreams.
Why then does her laughter cease
when the music stops?

Undated, approx. 1980's

TRUE VINE COMMUNITY

A Chapter in my Life

Middle Pocket was a hamlet.
"Beulah" a tiny farmhouse,
in the middle of paddocks,
strewn with ample cow dung,
drying in the scorching sun.
A creek running through it,
thorny blackberries bordering it.
A mouse once popped out of a drain,
in the middle of my shower!
All around neighbours,
living the alternate lifestyle.
Growing veggies,
harvesting fresh chicken eggs,
spinning and weaving,
and looking the part!
Walking home after a visit,
on a deserted country road,
pitch black and moonless,
except for the generous spread
of a crystal clear Milky Way
and its cohort.
Drenching rain, at times
caused creeks to overflow,
submerging bridges.
Surrounded by water-
house-bound!

Children celebrating,
"No school today!
Neither tomorrow,
till the waters subside."
Dave, a tall lanky Canadian,
with the most likeable laughter;
I was smitten straightaway.
Les the pastor,
a mixture of Jesus
and a gentle Indian guru,
attentive in conversation.
Plenty of young single mums
and their children,
sharing houses.
We felt safe and nurtured.
Many young married couples.
A few single men.
Sadly, no grey crowns,
to add needed life experience.
Most, from a hippy background;
once growing and smoking dope,
vegging out in Nimbin
and surrounds.
Our own school,
part of the church setup.
Many, encouraged to volunteer
one day a week.
Visiting the hills of Mullum,
a sudden revelation
of a process occurring in me,
which I defined later
as "group-think";
a "them and us" mind-set.

Alarm bells going off
in my mind.
The lingering stench
of cultism,
later quickly forgotten,
only to return with a vengeance,
when a bomb was dropped.
Suddenly, all leaders disbanded,
replaced by those from the city.
A new and unknown bunch.
Sheep scattered to the four winds.
Some returned to their old ways.
I moved house, withdrew,
and wrote poetry.
There I met a couple;
leaders in hiding,
wounded by dysfunction
in their church.
A different church.
And I quickly grew up.

11 October 2013

WAITING

Where is that someone,
not just anyone?
Free,
untangled,
mature,
ready
to make our relationship
a priority.

Recognizing
and fully aware
that such a relationship
and commitment
is what he wants,
even longs for.
Awake to the price
and willing to pay it.

While waiting,
I will fill my mind
and heart
with Him,
the Giver of all good things,
who gives bread to the hungry
and water to the thirsty.
Time is in His hands.

January 1993

WITHOUT A VOICE

A child abandoned.
Carers, too busy to hear
the crying in the night.
Without comfort,
eventually,
the crying ceased-
a hopeless giving up.
Left without a voice.

The little child, perceived to be
not too little to be left alone.
Detected by a roaming predator.
Beguiled by interest shown,
then entrapped by a web of threats.
The horror and defilement
by filth personified.
Left without a voice.

The fragile balance lost.
Threats echoing.
Fear in the field
and fear at night.
Tortured dreams.
Drawing pictures perverse.
Can anybody hear her silent screams?
Left without a voice.

Adults too busy
to cope with her obvious needs.
No one to show her
how to resolve those painful things.
All she gets is blame
and its resultant shame.
Unawares, she swallows that bitter pill.
Left without a voice.

Tossed like a rag-doll
from home to home.
Tolerating her,
as long as it suits them.
No one to take responsibility,
nor to make the commitment
to offer the warmth of a stable home.
Left without a voice.

The last attempt at care
consists of a regime of ridicule,
whenever she voices her thoughts.
Whether it be some issue at school
or bullies waiting on her way home,
the reply usually consists of blame,
reinforcing her sense of abandonment.
Left without a voice.

Time has passed.
She is now fifty-eight.
Why is she feeling so low tonight?
There have been triggers.
Voices from the past.
Is that how she used to feel?
Does this feeling have a name?
Yes, left without a voice!

Zurich, Switzerland
5 November 2005

YOU AND I

Two cliffs,
separated by a chasm-
you and I.
The chasm, fear.
You,
driven by the old fear
of not being loved.
Demanding
tokens of love.

As if that would satiate!
My fear:
being deprived of the freedom
to love freely.
Instead,
the heavy weight of expectations,
robbing joy in giving.
The risk is too great for you;
by letting go of control
you might end up
with nothing at all!
You cling to the illusion
that this will ensure
the quenching of thirst.
Sadly,
all you will ever get
is an unsteady trickle.
To get a gushing stream:
fear replaced
with appreciation-
trusting and embracing
my right to learn
to love you freely.

Easter 2002

Part 3

SPIRITUALITY

Finding the way out of the maze

FOREWORD

Psalm 73:26 "My body and mind may waste away, but God remains the foundation of my life and my inheritance forever." (GOD'S WORD® Translation)

The sub-title of this book of poetry summarizes my life experience and the above Scripture confirms it. My heart often failed and still fails me at times but my spirit is daily growing stronger.

I hope you, dear reader, will find this booklet refreshing, both to mind and body and strengthening to your spirit. I believe it speaks to people of all ages and walks of life. My aim and delight is to instill hope to the weary and increased courage, in order to face this thing called life.

None of us have chosen to be put on this earth but as we are now here, we may as well make the most of it by investing our time and focus wisely. You may be sitting in a prison cell, or some other kind of prison, or living it up (bored maybe of it?); the time is now! My struggles have been many but once, at rock bottom, I remember saying to myself: "It can only go up from here on!" and living it as if I meant it!

The greatest surprise for me has been to discover that the whole universe is permeated by a benevolent, yet powerful Spirit, who is eager to be found and to help us become the best we can be! This is a hidden truth, discovered mainly on a personal level, although by countless millions already. Evil is of course what is most apparent in our world.

At the back of this book you will find my author website details. I would love to hear how my book has impacted you.

A PICTURE OF THE VINEYARD

I saw a vineyard
at the time of harvest.
The vines were at their best,
heavy with big succulent grapes.
Their bowing branches
secured with man-made supports.

The vineyard was a picture of perfection.
Green leaves, in beautiful contrast
with round, deep purple grapes,
against a background of azure sky,
sprinkled with white fluffy clouds.
The world could stand still now!

Then came the harvesters,
cutting off the precious clusters,
gathering them in large baskets
and bringing them to the pressing vats.
The air filled with singing
and excitement at the good yield.

I became dismayed,
as the vine was gradually stripped
of its precious and beautiful yearly harvest.
So much patience producing that glorious fruit!
Glad of the outcome,
yet sad at the ensuing devastation.

Then the shocking realization
that the perfectly formed fruit,
lovingly tended by sun, rain
and human hands,
was to be crushed
into an awful pungent paste!

The Owner of the vineyard
is not aiming for the fruit itself.
He has a different purpose in mind.
In order to achieve the excellence of wine,
the fruit needs to be transformed,
by becoming a living sacrifice.

3 September 2005

ABIDING

Show me Lord
how to keep a soft heart,
without breaking my heart.

Show me Lord
how to keep a soft heart,
without hardening my heart,
as a defense.

Show me Lord
How, with this soft heart,
not to hold onto pain
until it brings forth death,
in the fruit of gloom.

Aware of people's hearts-
your response,
neither hardness nor gloom.
Instead, love and compassion,
while abiding in the Father;
your own heart resting safe and secure.

Show me Lord,
how to keep a soft heart-
by abiding in You.

Early 1980's

ANCIENT MANUSCRIPTS DECLARE

Ancient manuscripts declare:
The One who put together
flesh and bones,
nerves and sinews,
brain and mind,
heart and soul;
who skillfully weaved the DNA,
each strand to form a different chain;
who established the chemistry of cells
and commissioned legions of T- soldiers,
putting to shame man's awkward attempts
at guarding homeostasis' original design;
this One, the ancients say,
not only excels in knowledge and wisdom;
He also has a passionate heart for all He created,
which He guards jealously!
Fully understanding and committed
to His creation's needs,
He is Lord, without lording it over them.
Rather, He wants to be known
as Abba, a tender, loving parent.
Showing, through nature-
one of his clearest tools-
just how much He cares.

Doting mother hen and her chicks,
and the fierceness of a mother bear with cubs,
to name just a few.
Most importantly,
Jesus Christ, His only Son,
on the cross.
Is it too hard then, to respond to Him
in wonder and simple adoration?

30 January 2010

BLEAK DAY

Silent walking
on a cold, bleak day.
Hands in my pockets,
collar rolled up.
Rainclouds racing,
grey ripples on the lake.
Bare trees,
their leaves
strewn across my path.

Memories
of a similar scene-
aimlessly searching
for the unknown.
Lost and driven,
tightness within.
Questioning,
was there a hiding place
from that dull inner ache?
Much to think about,
so few answers!
The usual conclusion:
keep walking...
I am still walking-
in wonder now.

16 December 2006
Greenwell Point, NSW

BLESSED

Lord, where are you? he cried.
I am desperate.
Where are you?
All he could see,
through the tears,
were the infinite starry skies.
So remote and cold.

Why are you silent
when I need you most?
Blind, these eyes! he thought,
for I cannot see Him.
Neither can I touch Him,
nor hear Him.
What a useless body!

Then: Lord,
it's all too hard.
I need to touch,
hear and
see you tonight!
After a while-
silent resignation.

It was then that he heard
a timeless, tender voice,
by-passing his natural senses.
A word spoken into his spirit.
"Blessed are those
who have not seen
and yet believe." (John 20:29)

(In memory of an actual event
in 1984)

CAGES

The world's cages,
locked within cages.
Attempts to escape
and promises of liberty, at best,
only ever change the cage.

All in cages
many don't see.
False beliefs blinding
glimmers of freedom.
Promises only ever partly fulfilled.

One cage treatment,
another sobriety,
try correction and probation.
If these don't work,
simply change your identity.

Entertainment and fun
are more subtle than all
but dump you the quickest.
Soon you find yourself
back in your cage.

The world continues spinning-
the cages rattle and squeak.
Discarded, golden keys of broken promises,
glistening in an arctic sun.
Piercing, the world's primeval scream.

End the poem here?
Revel in hopeless despair?
More real, maybe?
Or more artistic that way?
So some would say!

I will frustrate
morose reality
and proudly state:
There is a counterpart
to human despair!

A master key
that opens all the locks.
Not shiny, nor golden,
but wooden, bloodstained
and in the form of a cross.

Written in 1992

CESSPOOL

Man's world-
a cesspool
of unrelenting chaos.
Man's will- jostling for control.
Man's thoughts-
messages in a bottle,
drifting on storm tossed seas.
Man's hunger-
big fish eating little ones.
Power and its pursuit
swallows up the one seeking it.
Those who find themselves
trusted leaders in the midst of all this,
easily become caught
in the quicksand of controversy.
The world would have you believe
that it is all about self!
The seas have become too small
for all those clamouring for a catch.
The truth isn't heard in the storm
nor in the frantic pace of life.
It requires drawing aside,
finding your own island,
returning to it often and persistently.
Becoming attuned
to that still small voice,
devoid of seduction or flattery.

The One who knows us as we are
welcomes us,
bringing refreshing and cleansing
and reminding us,
to our great relief,
that it is all about Him and His ways.
This is to be our focus,
our anchor,
as we seek to serve Him,
in His name,
in the cesspool of a drifting world.

10 September 2013

CHAMELEON

Through practice and necessity,
the chameleon has learned to mimic
every variation of its surroundings.
A master at concealment,
does it care about its true identity?

Its adaptation to stick and stone
and the in-built capacity to change its hue;
fascinating and puzzling indeed!
The underlying reasons;
protection and to fool its prey.

Among humans, a counterpart;
those that deftly project
what self-interest would demand.
Adapting their words and deeds
to what cunning dictates.

Some, like chameleon,
do it unawares;
a learned response
they picked up early in life,
like puppets on a string.

You find these chameleons
in every sphere of life,
piously sitting in church pews,
or else running big corporations,
charm a common disguise.

Do they care about their true identity?
Do they ever ask themselves:
what am I really here for,
apart from looking out for number one?
What bliss to find that God-given true self!

Written approx. 1979
(re-written 2016)

COCOON

(Joshua 5:13-15)

Inside this cocoon,
cosy and safe,
at times
the urge,
even need
to move my wings.
Mostly though,
comfortable
to just stay put.

Lately,
restlessness
and dissatisfaction,
living in the cocoon.
Dreaming of sailing
under stormy skies,
driven by strong currents,
daring to face
unknown dangers.

Longing to join brave hearts,
engaged in this holy war;
to release captives,
dying in their cocoons,
as well as wounded prey.
To be part of the holy assembly,
gathered around the Great Captain.
To become acquainted with His battle plans,
equipped with His armour and weapons of war.

I will continue breaking out.
Comfort now a prison.
On and on
this dream is driving me.
Little by little,
the walls are giving way.
The risk of what may be
and dangers assured:
a price I am willing to pay.

                                                7 December 2001

CONSTRICTION

Over the years,
a shriveling,
a constriction of the heart.
The hand once opened
has tightened its grip.
Instead of scattering seeds,
careful additions and subtractions.
The ardour of dreams,
given way
to dull compromise.
Soberness regarding self
and others,
mingled with short bursts of panic,
camouflaged behind a veil of busyness.
Experience has added skills
in the art of appearances
and deepened isolation.
So many comforts needed
to silence the crying heart!
Turning away from self,
hope is found
or rediscovered.
By opening one's heart,
just a little,
one steps into the road to life.

30 December 1993

CONTEMPLATING MORTALITY

Tear-filled waves of mortality
sweeping over me.
What appeared a challenge,
now a mere reminder of struggle
and increasing frailty.
A need to come away and reflect,
to process the shifting reality
of life's present stage.
For a time,
to contemplate a broken past.
What to keep and treasure?
What to let go,
to wrap in grave shroud and to bury?
Only then,
to direct my gaze
to what lies ahead.

Fleeing for a while
from self-imposed demands,
and needs for constant care.
To-do lists, my daily diet
(a daily obsession?).
Presently, I look around me–
this little caravan, once a delight.
Like me now,
showing signs of wear and tear.
Ants have taken up residence,
letting me know- I don't belong!

A spider weaved its web
in a new gap of the broken seal,
letting the rain in;
leaving behind stains and mould.
Decay setting in here too...

It seems that I have bitten off
more than I can chew.
A residue of past irresponsibility,
due to a then inability
to rightly assess situations,
people,
strengths and weaknesses
and making decisions accordingly.
Pain dealt with,
by substituting it
with a virtual world,
which tended to jar
with what was.
All reinforcing the habit
of living in unreality.
Eventually, tired of living a lie.

Now a thought, as quick as a flash:
"what gives value to my present life"?
"The people who allow me to love them?"
A still small voice within adds:
"Not just those you choose
but also those I send to you."
This is the new challenge:
not trying to prove anything.
A death knell to womanly bravado!

Just a niggling, yet liberating request
to live the life He has called me to,
though previously, amply proven a failure,
except to do it, moment by moment,
by faith in His enabling Love.
My weakness, frailty and mortality
now surrendered to His strength.

Wyee Point, NSW
10 November 2014

CORRIDORS

locked doors
empty corridors
walls white
shiny and sterile
hollow screams

words
echoing
towering
barricading
imploding

on a door
Love
and
No Admission
Need, not the password

the robot hand of loneliness
monotonously
and repetitive
reaches out-
you're back in your cell

4 October 1981

COUNT BLUEBEARD

Once again,
I have turned the key
to that forbidden room.

Anew,
staring
upon bloody, severed heads.

Despite myself,
becoming an accomplice
in the heinous deeds of rage.

This time,
I made a pact
with the One who keeps vigil.

Preceding-
fearless and honest confession
of violent words.

In future,
refraining
from entering Bluebeard's domain.

In times of pressure,
running to the Guardian instead.
The key- in His safekeeping!

                                12 March 2005

COVERINGS

Humans
find it very difficult
to acknowledge nakedness,
especially before our Creator.

Like those first parents,
we rush to cover ourselves
with man-made coverings-
inadequate at best.

Endless disputes continue,
igniting countless wars.
Inter-personal
and pandemic blame abounds.

That false covering-
originating in pride,
hiding toxic shame,
in order to present whole.

The lie acknowledged:
one step towards true wisdom.
Offered instead, is an adequate Covering,
ensuring true and lasting peace.

30 January 2016

DRIFTING

Strange and eerie-
a ship that's lost direction;
drifting
in the midst of the sea,
tossed about
by wind and waves.

Imperfect and frail,
any sense of self gone,
with no going back.
Bridges burned.
The future
uncertain and bleak.

Excitement for new things
vainly pursued.
Past hopes-
a smoldering pile of ashes.
Exhortations and pep-talks-
too hollow to hear.

Though rudderless,
on an ocean of lost dreams;
nevertheless,
my vessel is sailing
firm and secure,
in the palm of His hand!

March 1993

EASTER REFLECTIONS

He loved us completely,
offering the ultimate price.
No seeming guarantee then
it would ever pay off.
Love driven by love.
Recklessly, risking His very all,
for love's sake.

A free act,
springing from a free choice.
Yet, also a response
to the call of the Father.
Proving that His will
is highly desirable-
its outcome worth dying for.

Looking briefly into the abyss of fear-
then exchanging fear with trust.
By committing Himself into the Father's care,
surrendering all personal power,
He released the miracle of resurrection.
His victory- inspiring millions to rise up
and, in His name, to love recklessly.

                                                          18 September 2003

EX NIHILO

This morning
on waking,
out of the blue,
the thought,
or rather
the question
arose:
Why
is the earth,
in its center,
a ball of fire?

Why
create it such?
I am struck,
once again,
at the wonder
of this Mind
who created our world
and the worlds
so perfect,
without a prototype,
rather– ex nihilo!

What a mind!
What a being!
Could one put together
all the wisdom of man,
in comparison,
it would be a mere drop
in the oceans of the world.

My reflection went further.
This incredible being
delights in being called Father,
by those who love Him.

He has prepared a kingdom,
a place for many to dwell,
walking and talking together with Him ,
in the cool of gardens of delight.
The only condition:
no contamination, through sin, to enter in.
Instead,
cleansing confession and baptism in water,
bowing to the kingship of His Son,
and only then to enter through the Door,
appointed by Him. (John 10:9)

21 November 2007

EXPRESSING THE INEXPRESSIBLE

Contemplating from my window
the new wonder of a sunrise,
amid the call of the Currawong,
I become aware once more-

You are my first impulse
to greet You,
each day
when I regain waking consciousness.

You are the sunlight that pierces through,
gradually dispelling the heaviness,
when in me
I discover a foggy greyness.

You are the Majestic Artist
who, ex nihilo, long ago
created goodness and beauty
and every day anew.

You remain in control
amidst seeming chaos and despair-
the eye of the storm
dwells in perfect calm.

You are the lofty One, the One enthroned.
The self-sufficient One.
Through Calvary,
wooing Your creation back to Yourself.

You are the One
Who freely chose to tie Yourself
with an everlasting oath, a covenant,
to the shiftiness of the human heart- my heart!

July 1994

FAITH vs. EXPECTATIONS

Today,
the sting of disappointment,
once again.

An outcome hoped for
perished and died,
once again.

What did I place my faith in?
Favourable circumstances,
once again?

Or was it in a certain outcome
involving a specific person,
once again?

Fickle human hope,
versus faith in something unshakable,
once again?

It is staggering to me;
the persistence of the same mistake,
once again!

Faulty thinking plaguing this representative
of the human race,
once again.

I awaken to the fact
that I am called to faith,
once again.

Somehow,
the penny doesn't seem to drop,
once again.

The concept of faith confused
with fickle, soulish expectations,
once again.

When the latter get dashed,
disappointment tries to steal even my faith,
once again.

I need the dividing scalpel of the Word;
A lie-ectomy of heart and mind,
once again.

Once removed and put on the altar,
God's consuming fire will deal with it –
once and for all!

17 February 2016

FAITH

Faith, like love-
usually misunderstood.
When spoken of,
one's own version perceived.

The faithful-
those
who together
uphold a common creed?

From mere observation,
while comfortable in safe detachment,
trembling, I took a leap...
of faith!

That very faith-
through and in the One,
opened a door to His Realm.
Newfound, all of Heaven's resources!

There is an age-old counterfeit,
weaving through fables,
myths and the occult,
promising power: dark and self-serving.

True faith,
given in order to love
and to do His will on earth-
part of our magnificent destiny!

Yet, even among those
said to have "ears to hear",
often an impotent understanding.
Birds that never leave their nests.

Surrounded by the earthbound,
it is risky to start flapping one's wings.
Our fragile egos bruised
by the consequences of practice.

Faith never guarantees instant success.
But act we must!
We have sure promises
from One who cannot lie.

12 July 2010

FIG LEAVES

Why insist
on wearing fig leaves,
when Father prepared
a covering, costly indeed?
It provides warmth,
beauty and restoration.
A covering for shame,
an invitation to the humble
to belong.

Instead,
we revel in our self-adequacy,
pouring contempt on dependence.
We point the finger
at the glaring faults of others
blind to see them in ourselves,
while failing to see
three more fingers
pointing back at us!

2 November 2007

FREE TO LOVE

Lord,
if there is one prayer
I pray above all else
it is this-
to be set free
from the tyranny
of my own needs,
the self-centeredness
of my petty frustrations,
the endless array
of wants and cravings-
in order to love
the unlovable,
like me.

To find the caring,
the courage,
the challenge,
in order to embrace
the broken-hearted-
despite my ripped out heart.
To focus instead
on hope and faith,
and to learn to trust You.
No longer
tossed to and fro,
due to fickleness.
LORD set me free
to love as You love me!

(Undated)

GENESIS AGAIN

*"The earth was without form, and void,
and darkness was on the face of the deep.
And the Spirit of God was hovering
Over the face of the waters." (Genesis 1:2)*

Plunged in darkness,
roaring arctic winds
sweep over earth's surface.
The howling spirit of the world
whipping up waves,
crowned with black foam.

Earth's positioning in the universe
to receive life from the sun
and steady watering from its ecosystem-
not yet in place.
Oversight by a skilled manager-
not yet fashioned from the earth.

Many unknown millenniums from there,
darkness once again covering the earth.
This time, due to the enemy's workings
and his successful takeover bid;
man, sacked from his job-
a hobo, sifting through the world's trash.

A rescue plan devised from the start,
despite the deepening darkness
of centuries of failure and sin.
The golden thread of a promise,
confirmed by prophets: God's Calvary.
Confounding to all.

That insignificant-looking shoot,
springing forth from a long-felled stump,
accomplished that second Genesis of man.
Darkness swallowed by the Light of the World.
The sure promise of walks anew,
in the cool of His gardens of delight.

30 November 2000

GOD'S RICHNESS

Manifold wisdom,
uncontainable,
past human comprehension.
As high as the sky is above the earth,
so high are His ways.
Only a fraction revealed,
reflected in creation.
Innumerable manifestations
of beauty and perfection,
evoking worship.
Unlimited generosity, freely shared.

Extravagant lover for love's sake.
Your arms are never full.
Countless, your thoughts towards us.
The treasury of your gifts- never exhausted.
Eternity barely contains
all that you have in store for us.
You delight to delight
and to enlarge the joyful giver-
to make room for the lonely.
You take the willing heart,
to reflect your own.

26 July 2012

HAY AND STUBBLE

Many words,
mere hype.
The greater the shallowness,
the louder the noise.

Wordiness,
to cover up lack.
Decorative words,
like peacock feathers.

Unless words
match actions
and actions
match words...

Mere sound waves,
tickling some ears.
Like rainless clouds;
hunger and thirst left untouched.

Words He calls
hay and stubble.
Destined
for the fire of His judgement.

August 1994

HE KNOWS

(Isaiah 49:2)

Presently,
in limbo.
Sharp pain arising
from the distant memory
of taking wings.

Living
in chosen confinement,
minimal space
and limited tasks-
the rigidity of discipline.

Apparently, the fastest,
most accurate arrows
are made from twisted,
gnarled and tortured
desert wood.

Drenched,
stretched,
methodically pinned down,
until finally
the end goal is reached.

Before,
seemingly useless
to the untrained eye.
Now, made dead straight
and excelling in springiness.

Knowing the Master's ways,
takes away quiet despair.
He is well acquainted
with my desire to fly,
his greater purpose I will trust.

Middle Pocket, NSW
16 August 1984

HIS GIFT

Days of relaxed pondering,
sensing His constant presence.
My van parked amidst empty sites.
Wind gusts in the trees, then pouring rain.
Soon, the blazing sun returns,
shadowed by intermittent racing clouds.

On weekends, the sites fill up:
families with kids,
noisily populating pools
and jumping atop rubber mounds.
Fishermen sitting around at night,
a little too jolly for sobriety.

My aloneness now a heavy garment,
conscious of it when I gaze out to sea,
watching bold surfers,
like corks in the distance.
A black dog, a friendly mutt,
racing up and down the beach.

He runs up to people,
while looking out concerned,
his master disappearing under waves.
Now near me, shaking himself, shivering,
turning around and whimpering,
cold from vainly joining his owner-

The weight is there too,
when walking along the beach;
a mum watching her kids playing
near the edge of the sea,
an animated group of friends
walking past me.

I look for treasures cast up by the sea,
quietly praying for a sign
of His constant presence.
A bright blue stone maybe?
A definite rarity
and worthy love token!

Yet, proofs of His love
already more than a few-
and I am chastened.
The next day I follow a path
around the Peninsula,
to the river's mouth.

Many smooth, multi-coloured stones
along its rocky shore.
A blue one?
I find blue chips,
fragments of shells,
but no blue stone.

Then-
a bright red coral catches my eye!
I bend down and pick it up;
although a-symmetric,
like the human heart,
that is exactly its shape!

Sculpted by a loving
yet invisible hand;
His tools:
sand, rocks, turbulent waters
and time.
My heart and spirit now singing!

27 November 2011
Crookhaven Heads

HIS TEMPLE

With a whip of cords,
He drives them all out.
"Take these things away!"
The Temple is His Body,
not built with human hands;
its building stones
made up by those
sealed with His Spirit.
Should the idols of sloth and greed,
lust and pride therefore
co-habit with His Spirit?
Zeal for the temple of God
still consumes Him. (John 2:3-12)

21 January 2016

HOUSE OF MIRRORS

The world– a house of mirrors,
wherein we live and move
and think we get our being from.
Born and raised
in the authority of the image,
projected by distorted mirrors,
in a daze,
we wander around the maze,
seeking the exit.

Away from conflict and contradiction,
we are driven by a knowing,
a longing for truth and simplicity;
where fragments fit
and missing pieces are found.
Where our mirror,
like a still mountain lake,
reflects an undistorted image:
His.

June 2008

IN HIM

"In Your light we see light"
(Psalm 36:9)

Also true:
in Your Truth
we see truth.

In Your Pain,
we accept pain
and are transformed.

In Your Wisdom,
we are able to discern
and to know wisdom.

In Your Righteousness,
we lay down our own
and are declared righteous.

In Your Holiness,
we are changed
to be more like You.

In Your Love
we come to know love
and become loving.

4 October 2016

IN HIS SAFE KEEPING – AT LAST!

That in-built heart's desire,
familiar to most,
that longing
for a true and lasting soul mate;
my greatest source of pain,
failure, shame and fear.
A dark shadow,
pursuing me.
A hidden snare,
repeatedly tripping me up,
entangling me-
delivering but a poor counterfeit.

Tonight, finally free
from this life-long search!
Surprised at how long it's taken me
to place this sorry saga
into the loving care of Abba Father.
His peace- A sure promise,
in exchange for my anxious striving.
No longer to give it any thought.
Should it once again try to arise,
I will continue reminding myself:
it is now out of my control
and in my loving Father's safe keeping.

29 January 2016

LIFE'S LEARNING

Funny how God,
in his patience,
honours the vows of him
who's never practiced faithfulness before.

Like setting out in a boat,
without having mastered navigation.
Allowing learning to occur on the fly.
I pity his companions!

Foolhardy-
by both navigator
and his crew.
Shipwreck most likely.

That's exactly what we do.
In love, we make our vows-
soon to be broken?
What was that all about?

People are needy,
from birth to the grave.
Character understands,
thinks through and only then commits.

Our God is such.
He ties Himself to us with an unbreakable vow,
knowing full well the state of our hearts.
Because of His heart, safe harbour is assured!

10 July 2010

LIFE'S LINK

Baby asks for it
in its crying.

The young child,
in his tantrums.

The metamorphic teenager,
in his defiance.

The young adult,
in his search for meaning.

The family man,
in his juggling.

The older man,
in his disillusionment.

The old man,
in his search for peace.

"Hesed": an aspect of Agape.
Love, that stems from God.

Fully displayed for us,
in the willing suffering of His Son.

7 July 2010

MIRRORS

In the midst of a noisy carnival,
a maze of mirrors; all with distortions.
Someone threw a rock-
reflected, a shattered world.
Fragments of differing beliefs;
the illusions of broken people.
Like stalls at universities' open days,
beckoning you to sign up.
The relativity of truth-
where you pick your own version.
Find the one that makes you happy,
from the smorgasbord of life.
Past heated debating;
eerie laughter echoing
from the master of the carnival.

When ready, step away.

Wander the lonely, deserted streets.

Feel the icy wind

blowing through your very core.

Head towards the desert.

Don't look back.

Throw away your soft drink

and your fairy floss;

only the clouds to distract you now.

Keep going,

for there is a well to be found,

fed by a spring, cool and crystal clear.

The ancient promise of thirst-quenching water.

As you bend down to drink,

you discover a mirror without flaws.

March 1996

MY BELOVED

My Beloved took me for a walk today.
He is an artist, superbly so.
He pointed out to me the endless hues,
the infinite variety of textures
and how He intermingles them.

He is the ultimate landscaper,
displaying expert division of space
into ever-changing sky,
undulating, wooded planes and meadows
and the restless, glistening and sparkling sea.

This, and so much more,
revealing His mind and heart,
overflowing with love to create,
to delight and to bless.
Endowed with perfect insight.

Although, what brought tears to my eyes
wasn't so much the display of His might,
but the heart of my Beloved
Who, although Lord of all,
made Himself Servant of all!

22 March 1984

MY SWITZERLAND

Church bells tolling,
solemnly marking time,
ringing throughout the cities.
Sentinels,
there to remind-
about Carpe Diem?
A national obsession maybe
with managing time?
If sentinels-
they have become
meaningless symbols!
The outward retained,
its truth detained
and locked away.

Nevertheless,
there is an undercurrent
gradually gaining momentum.
A controversial oddity,
a powerful groundswell,
growing in strength
from above.
A hidden chrysalis,
mostly secure in its cocoon,
watched over by Love.
Already though,
the emergence of new creations.
True sentinels,
heralding the wake-up call!

Zürich, Switzerland
12 October 2005

NECESSARY DISILLUSIONMENT

I used to think that the biblical saying
"the heart is desperately wicked"
was at best an exaggeration,
at worst- the description of my own heart.

Lately,
searching for my deeper motives
for seemingly good deeds,
asking for the truth to be revealed.

I soon find
instead of love,
sometimes,
the motive lies in guilt.

Also in insincerity,
inferiority,
in needing to be needed,
to feel good.

What about
to be seen as good,
to prove that I am the strong one?
And the list goes on...

His glory said to dwell in earthen vessels.
As long as I attempt to look good,
to seem loving beyond reproach,
all that is seen is a whitewashed vessel.

Only when that vessel
is allowed to crack and chip,
can the precious contents
finally seep through.

13 May 2008

NEW WORLD

Are you dreaming of a world
where truth, love and peace
can be trusted?
Where the things
that your heart longs for,
are a rock under your feet
and not quicksand,
as you may be experiencing?

Do you ask yourself,
how can I be loving
and really truthful,
without being taken advantage of
and eaten alive?
You would like to trust,
yet rightly fear
wishful thinking.

From painful experience you know
the world to be hard as nails.
Instead of love- exploitation.
Instead of truth- compromise.
Instead of peace- unceasing striving.
Worse still:
these very things
have now become part of you also.

Torn and tossed between the two;
the wrestle is uneven.
Your dream and hope
for what ought to be-
like a child
wrestling with an adult.
Eventually, some let the child go to sleep,
or forcefully send him to his room.

The One who calls Himself Truth still speaks:
"Seek (and keep on seeking),
and you will find.
Knock, (and keep on knocking),
and the door will be opened onto you." (Matt. 7:7)
This promise stands as dependable
as the rising of the sun each day,
for the One who spoke can be trusted!

                            Undated (timeless maybe?)

ON MY WAY TO WORK

A day
like any other working day.
Making my way
through the usual city crowd,
in order to get to work.
Then,
out of the blue,
this awesome presence
which seems to envelop me.
A presence
so warm,
so kind,
so reassuring...
Like an embrace
from a loving father,
or what I imagine
a loving father to be like.
He seems to say:
"You belong."
"You are part of Us."
"You are loved and cherished."
I struggle to hold back the tears.
Tears of joy and gratitude!
I've waited all my life to hear those words!
Presently, my smile turns into a grin-
I realize that, for a moment,
I actually forgot where I work!

23 December 2003

OUR MAGNIFICENT DESTINY

How subtly
the enemy moves.
We know it,
yet do we perceive?

Individualism, through ease,
defines how we live and are.
We see it as a fact,
fail to see it as a curse.

Our togetherness-
a weak expression of His love.
Our destiny- to move as one in Him.
Our preconditioned minds- unable to see.

For we do not need each other,
though we say we do.
Keeping ourselves separate,
and therefore living ineffectively.

When dulling ease is far removed,
we may recognize our need of one another.
We then will move together,
to fulfil our magnificent destiny!

12 July 2010

PARADISE

How can we seek after Paradise,
without seeking its Creator and Sustainer?
Yet, we do it all the time!
Each one pursuing,
or attempting to create
our own version of paradise.
The poor seek the paradise of plenty.
The oppressed- freedom and power.
The greedy- wealth and indulgence.
The ugly- beauty that opens doors of favour.
The naive- the false promise of dazzling riches,
simply by finding the right know-how.
The illusion, perpetrated throughout the ages,
of paradise for us alone,
where we will find eternal bliss,
living happily ever after.
A tailor-made lie,
prepared for each one of us,
keeping us busy for a lifetime,
in pursuit of that lost Eden.
Never was there a lie
so effective for generations past
and generations yet to come.
A dangling carrot,
always out of reach.
That shimmering Fata Morgana,
dissolving into the ether,
as soon as you seem to reach it.

I am convinced-
paradise is not a place,
nor a state of being
but rather-
a person:
Jesus Christ His name.
(Ephesians 1:3)

25 February 2016

PRAYER

God of love,
teach me
to continue walking
in love,
continuing to give
and to receive
love.

Especially
when knocked back,
when doors slam closed.
When I bump against
my own limitations and fears,
let me not be like the snail
that retreats in its shell.

God of love,
teach me
to continue walking
in love,
continuing giving
and receiving your Love,
through others.

10 September 1994

PRISONS

Many kinds of prisons;
some made of wood and iron bars
with iron doors and deadbolts,
some within relationships
and the obsessive fear of loss.

The worst kind-
the self-imposed ones.
Those keeping us trapped
in a box labelled "inadequacy",
binding us with cords of shame.

Careful to hide
our real self,
with its brokenness,
its insecurities and failures,
behind a façade of make-belief.

The self-imposed prison door
will freely release its captor-
the key that must be used
is in the shape of a cross,
its name tag: Agape.

19 March 1993

RESTLESS

Chasing time.
Filling void?
Living
according to rules.
Whose?
Failed expectations
or deliberate failure?
Friends with half smiles-
lukewarm?
Unable to give
beyond their ease?
Am I one of them?
Probably, at times!
Impulse buying-
a cupboard full of clothes
not quite matching.
To and fro,
swings the pendulum.
Peace,
only found
when I cease running
from resting in You.

21 June 1994

RISEN

The Prince of Life
chose to wrestle with death;
a battle so fierce,
a conflict so great-
defeat appeared complete.

Like a surfer,
disappearing
under a monster wave.
A boxer,
knocked out in the ring.

Death seemed
to have swallowed him up,
while all of Heaven stood stricken.
The Father,
shedding silent tears.

Yet,
just like the surfer,
rising from under the wave,
the boxer facing another round-
death could not hold Him down!

He is risen,
once and for all!
The Father's tears,
tears of joy and pride
in His victorious Son.

20 November 2007

SCAPEGOAT

The Shepherd of the sheep
heard the lonely cries
of the scapegoat,
driven into the wilderness.
It had been sent there,
carrying other people's sins-
condemned because of them.

He came and rescued me.
Washed me clean of all sins;
theirs and mine, imputed upon me.
Of their judgements,
rejection and condemnation.
Of their decree to dwell in the wilderness
and to roam in arid places.

He has brought me to green pastures
and made me lie near still waters.
He invites me to enjoy His abundance
and to dance amongst the spring lambs.
He has flooded me with His acceptance
and invited me to partake of His Truth-
gradually washing away the lies of the past.

23 November 1996

SEA OF TEARS

Three thirty in the morning
and I'm awake,
in a flood of tears.
The weight of memories,
of irreplaceable losses
and cruel betrayals-
I find myself drowning!

Before this wave of sadness
carries me away,
rudderless,
should I reach for those tablets again?
Get down on my knees
and pray
a prayer of desperation?

I walk to the kitchen
for a comforting drink.
Slowly, becoming conscious
of other struggling lives.
No longer alone now,
I share the sadness and tears
of mankind itself.

This place- a sea of tears,
where broken people
break anew
and are broken by others.
Clinging to fragments
of their shattered dreams,
hoping to be saved from oblivion.

There is a Boatman
and his crew.
Their mission;
to save us from drowning
and to heal our brokenness,
wrapping us in garments of praise
and wiping away every tear (Revelation 21:4).

                                              11 September 2012

SHELTER FROM THE STORM

That cosy cabin,
a shelter from the storm,
could have become
my permanent abode,
had it not been
for a call
to go higher,
to venture out
into the howling tempest,
facing the headwind
and the icy gale.
One last glance back,
shedding a tear of regret.

Then facing onward and upward,
my Faithful Companion
by my side,
to strengthen,
guide
and direct my footsteps,
amidst the mist
and surrounding shrouds of fog.
On treacherous terrain,
till we reach that final destination;
the Palace on High,
where pasture lands abound
and where rivers of life
and calm waters
forever restore the soul.

17 December 2015

SHUTDOWN

In a world,
where man has become
its coincidental final link,
in a purposeless chain of events,
man's thoughts resound
in the draughty corridors of time.
Munchean shadows, screaming,
erratically hastening along,
driven by collective angst,
stooped over by invisible burdens,
searching for existential meaning
and vainly attempting to make sense
of a seemingly senseless universe.

We superimpose bigger telescopes
onto our distorted vision
and fail to perceive the singular,
in relation to the whole.
Shut down the telescopes.
Huddle down in some cave,
out of the gale,
away from all the babble.
Close your eyes
and take a deep breath.
Slowly, a single word will surface;
Help!
And the universe breathes a sigh of relief.

Zurich, Switzerland
9 July 1998

SIMPLICITY

Less talk– more silence.
Less things– more time.
Less action– more focus.
Less friends– more friendship.
Less getting– more giving.
Less fear– more trust.
Less of man– more of God.

9 October 1997

SURVIVAL DEMANDS IT

Two ways only
to live on this earth.
The majority-
big fish
eating little ones.
Hunger must be fed.
Needs-
many and varied.
Some- more wants
than needs.

Charm-
to attract,
then entrap.
Spiders,
weaving their webs,
using sources of light
for their own purpose.
Power-
to satisfy the illusion
of control.

"Come onto me..."
the Shepherd calls to the sheep.
Unlike entrepreneurial farmers,
merely throwing bales of hay
into the thronging fold.
Rather,
tenderly and watchfully,
hand-fed,
each one known
by its name.

Sheep,
dwelling peacefully,
harmlessly,
in pastures green
and abundant,
beside the still waters.
Without need
for cunning guile,
in order to thrive
and survive.

4 October 2016

THE ALTAR OF THE LIE

From the womb,
she was trained
and branded
by the dark angel
who guards the prison
of the lonely.

Throughout life,
groomed by abandonment,
betrayal,
abuse and neglect;
tried and tested methods
of recruitment.

Early,
she was taught
to worship at the altar of the lie.
To undergo ceremonial cutting
and to endure continuous bleeding.
Wounds that would not heal.

So far,
many sacrificial offerings:
authentic values in exchange
for superficial relief.
Genuine identity
for others' perception of self.

As for now,
the story could end there
but doesn't.
The prison door
has released its captive.
The healing journey has begun.

The altar-
finally smashed!
Life's ashes,
in exchange for beauty.
Her pain of loneliness
soothed by the balm of trust.

26 June 2005

THE ARTFUL DODGER

During my recent travels,
I met a puzzling group.
Gathering in nobly appointed gardens,
sharing refined cuisine,
conducting thoughtful conversations,
displaying great insight
into the manifold world of knowledge
and exalting those among themselves,
at the forefront of such exchange.
When questioned,
some humbly confessed to deeds,
done and being done
under the banner of charity,
wearing them like a glittering diadem.

In hindsight,
just as prone to his schemes,
I nevertheless could sense
the artful dodger's presence.
Always cleverly disguised
through ceaseless trickery
and clever deception.
His mission:
to promote avoidance of the call,
given by the Master Himself.
The call for the seed to fall to the ground,
and to die,
in order to bear lasting fruit,
useful and pleasing to Him (John 12:24).

17 June 2012

THE DAM

In a vision,
I saw a dam
filled with water.
Sometimes,
the retaining wall would part
and the water would gush forth.
Then,
it would close again
and no water would flow.

I know,
the dam was my heart.
The one operating the dam-
the self, my self,
using my will
and limited understanding,
my emotions,
often triggered
by my circumstances.

I now earnestly desire
to hand over
the control of this dam
to my Lord and friend.
He will open those walls
and leave them permanently so-
allowing the water to flow
unhindered,
as He would want.

11 November 1984

THE FINAL VERDICT

You talk to me of war,
as a yardstick of truth.
You mention the Warsaw ghetto,
the war in Vietnam,
the situation in Palestine,
the present plight in Iraq
and other seemingly senseless events.
You use them to support your beliefs
in man's predominant darkness
and in the universe's journey towards chaos.
All things, you say,
are moving towards destruction.
Death, to you, is the final harvest
of all living things.

You have gathered your evidence,
weighed up the arguments,
and you have made a final verdict.
Will you not stop
and reconsider
re-opening the trial...?
You have presented
only one side of the story.
All these things are true-
darkness is everywhere.
Man's evil ever present.
Due to your chosen world view,
your focus is fixed on evidence
supporting the conclusion you made.

Despite what you and I may believe-
the ultimate verdict,
resounding throughout creation,
has been spoken from above:
*"The light shines in the darkness,
and the darkness did not overcome it."*
(John 1:3)
I venture to add,
this was accomplished
because of another word,
spoken from a cross:
*"Father forgive them,
for they know not what they do."*
(Luke 23:34)

                                                  1 August 2004

THE GOLDEN CUP OF POISON

I can feel the consequence
of tasting poison
in that sparkling cup.
My spirit wilting,
curled up in an embryonic state.
My soul mournful,
my body limp,
my mind fluctuating
between ceaseless action
and mindless inertia.
I am hiding away
in my cocoon,
which fails to soothe me,
due to its lapsed due-by-date.

Drawing my attention away
from inner brokenness,
my present state-
that of a self-righteous spinster,
full of jealous disdain
towards those who would tackle life.

20 July 1996

THE GREAT WEDDING FEAST

Before Eden,
the Father dreamed a dream
for His Only Begotten Son.

Just like in Song of Songs,
The Bridegroom
still seeking His bride.

A bride without blemish,
tested in the fire of affliction,
coming forth pure as gold.

His wooing began at a wedding.
It will reach its completion
at the Great Wedding Feast.

The Spirit, the Groom's best man,
has made Himself available
for the Groom's every beck and call.

The invitations are still going out.
The banqueting table is being set.
The bride is being made ready for that day.

November 2011

THE GREATEST GIFT OF ALL

Who doesn't know that Christmas
is a time to give and to receive
marvelous and not so striking gifts?
A time to make peace
with self and our fellow man.
A time to make contact
with those long neglected.
Last but not least,
a time to give out
a little human kindness,
to spread unreserved happiness
and to put a joyous glow
on someone's face.

Yet, year after year,
in very many homes,
the same unobtrusive Gift
remains unopened
and forgotten,
under the Christmas tree.
The Giver,
going through the same sadness,
year after year,
that His Gift has been ignored
or worse; even scorned.
"How could this be?", you may ask.
"Am I doing the same?"

Those gifts,
so central to this Season,
a symbol of the greatest Gift of Love:
a heartbroken Father's giving
of His Only Begotten Son,
in order to redeem His rebellious
and wayward children unto Himself.
By candlelight, we sing the songs,
we pray the prayers,
remembering Him, "Light of the world".
Like children, admiring the gifts under the tree
but never unwrapping His.
This Christmas, maybe?

Undated (sometime in the 80's)

THE IDEALIST

A gift or a curse-
this ability to perceive,
so clearly,
the image, the outline
of the ideal?

The present
jars against that image,
leaving a painful sense of lack
and the compulsion to conform
to the ideal.

This passion- always there!
Like a superimposed grid
or a builder's plumb line;
setting the standard
of the ideal.

There's a need to adjust
two fields of vision
to one single image,
making peace with what is
and the ideal.

The Master Optician
knows the adjustment required.
His vision tenderly embraces
both what is,
as well as His ideal.

23 March 1998

(Interestingly, this poem was written one day before an appointment with an optician, who diagnosed me with a "Muscular Eye Convergence Disorder"!)

THE MEANING OF LIFE

The meaning of life...
What life?
Whose life?
What meaning?
Whose meaning?

Isn't life
simply for living?
The meaning-
a quest
beyond our scope?

Why then the abused?
The handicapped?
The rich?
The poor?
And all those at war?

Why this insatiable yearning
for love,
for truth,
for security,
for power?

It is driving us,
mercilessly,
on a seemingly endless quest,
till finally,
we break in despair.

The meaning of life-
so many unanswered questions!
Life reduced to mere existence.
Could its meaning be
that there is meaning!

Undated

(An ageless question?)

THE MYTH OF SELF-SUFFICIENCY

For a while,
I carry on
my usual lifestyle.
Trying to achieve
most of my goals,
the essential ones first.
Then,
gradually arising in me,
emptiness.
I push harder,
ignoring the ache;
the desire for a lover,
some friendly company,
even a cry on someone's shoulder.

Finally,
I sit down,
unsuccessful
in turning a deaf ear
to that insistent plea.
Frustration and helplessness,
anger and guilt ensue,
subsiding to stark perception.
I am not,
as the false self
would like me to believe,
a self-sufficient being
but vulnerable,
due to inner need.

Past attempts
all have fallen short
at stilling the yearning.
A cruel farce?
A sadistic streak
permeating creation?
The reflection
of the character
of its architect?
Presently arising,
a glimmer of understanding.
The wonder and discovery
of purposed dependency
upon a wooing Creator.

April 1992

THE ONE ESSENTIAL THING

(Galatians 2:22)

The one essential thing
required of us,
which demands least action
but is the hardest of all,
is something hardly ever taught.

Instead, our religious selves
never tire listening
to countless methods
of how to improve
and ennoble the self.

We piously pray for more patience,
to overcome our impatient selves.
Or else, we clothe ourselves in sackcloth,
on Mondays, after week-end excess,
resuming the cycle again, Fridays.

We adopt loving mannerisms,
in order to gain favour.
We seek status within our circles
and call it "walking in authority"-
a far cry from the Master's example!

That one essential thing,
without which we simply are deluded,
is the insight and willingness
to consider the striving, religious self
utterly unable to please God.

Unless we recognize the need,
to allow the Spirit to include us in Christ's death,
to daily pick up that cross of death to self,
we will be content to play the religious game-
never knowing the wonder of a resurrected life in Him.

> Culburra Beach,
> 28 January 2016

THE PARABLE OF FIRE

The Teacher's favourite way
to impart spiritual reality
was through parables.
He still speaks through them-
using stones, loaves of bread, or even fire.

Today, I forced my overactive mind
to become still,
while watching dancing flames.
Man and fire;
an ancient and vital partnership!

I noticed some of the wood
starting to smoke-
burned only in part.
When pushed back into the center,
the smoke ceased.

One log even fell out of the fireplace,
as if to emphasize this truth.
Struggling to place it back,
I noticed its glow subside,
causing profuse smoke.

Removed from the center,
without its fire,
it became a mere nuisance.
Even coal, without the flame,
remains just a black piece of char.

20 May 2003

THE RELIGIOUS SELF

I love my spiritual life.
It enhances my demeanour,
refines some of my impulses
and puts me in touch with good people.

Much sharing for me occurring.
I have something to say.
I am heard and valued.
My goals are supported.

Help is given to me
to achieve my dreams.
In turn, I feel generous,
when helping others.

I have something to give
which makes me feel important.
God is giving me abundant life
to enjoy with my family and friends.

I am called blessed by all.
No need for me to struggle.
No need for me to be in pain.
This is His ultimate will for me.

The religious self is all about ME! *(John 3:30)*

16 January 2016

THE TEMPLE

(In memory of the past meditation temple
at Homelands Community, Upper Thora, NSW)

In a secluded place,
with wooded surrounds,
the picturesque Bellinger river nearby-
a graceful yet simple wooden temple,
roofed and open on three sides,
handcrafted mats for comfort.
A place to meditate,
to contemplate the surrounds,
to listen to the singing river,
crickets and birds,
even your own voice!

Thai Chi, taught
and practiced by Roger,
a seeker after spiritual truth.
We had some wonderful talks.
An earnestness about him,
integrity, wholesomeness
and striving after excellence
were expressions of his being.
Strangely,
in his presence
I felt like an awkward child.

He commented once,
disappointed and annoyed,
how little appreciation for the sacred
some visitors seemed to have.
Happy to visit the place,
but not caring to leave it
as they found it.
Instead,
littering with soft drink cans,
cigarette butts and papers;
their unimpressive visiting cards.

That temple, its guardian and visitors
still strike a chord within me,
though part of a different era in my life.
It now represents a sanctuary to me,
spanning across many faiths and philosophies.
A place, symbolizing that primal need in man
to connect with that Great Being
I now call Abba Father.
That process
and the appreciation thereof;
the very thing that sanctifies a temple.

27 November 1990

THE UNIVERSAL FOUNT

I am staying in a van park,
boasting great and majestic trees.
A hill on one side, a lake on the other.
Manicured lawns and flowers everywhere-
a mini-community!
Residents who own their homes-
some, perched right over the lake,
overlooking expansive waters.
Others, backing onto the bush.
Great pride evident everywhere
in one's own little piece of haven.

In the van opposite, an elderly couple,
speaking a foreign tongue.
The man, working outside
nearly all day long,
even in the heat of day.
Small jobs it seems.
At the end of the day,
I cannot tell
what changes he has made.
Occasionally, the woman appears,
hands on hips.

I wish I could go over and ask:
Are you happy here?
Is this how you want to live,
or are you bored?
Maybe not enough to do?
Don't you know that the world
needs people like you?

Not too busy with survival,
nor living up to the Jones.
For who else will care for those
who cannot care for themselves?

Let me tell you about Mary,
sitting all day in a chair– rocking.
Stopped, through locks and restraints,
from wandering off.
Light comes into her eyes
when someone sits down and talks to her,
occasionally patting her hand.
There's Billy, who can't stop stealing.
His friends only pay attention
when he offers to pay.
Standing alone before the sentencing judge.

These are just a few of the people,
all around us.
So many, doing it tough.
Being there for others
taps into the spiritual law
that "it is more blessed to give
than to receive".
Simply, because in giving
we keep open
the fount of receiving,
ensuring that it flows freely.

10 November 2002

TIME ALONE

Time to get away.
I am packing the bare minimum,
ensuring that pen and paper,
and my favourite books
are included,
along with the rest.
What I will wear
does not matter.
I only need to please myself.
Glorious freedom,
just to sit or walk,
to read and write.
No need to talk, except,
like silent breathing,
to the One who always listens,
and to listen
to the One
who always speaks.

December 2004

WAKING FROM STUPOR

How does the world
make sense of faith?
A biased view,
possibly philosophical in nature?
A personal obsession
or a favourite hobby,
indulged in on Sundays,
or when saying table grace?
Spiritual symbolism,
expressed in religious ritual,
stemming from man's existential angst-
a lingering residue of primitive man?
Nothing, to be sure,
assisting or of relevance
with the day to day issues of modern life?
Perception's eccentricities,
best kept private and to oneself?

In order to avoid the ridicule and rancour
of society's imposition of its silent norms,
at times, I have attempted to comply,
out of hunger for acceptance,
or fear of loss of pseudo esteem,
even from sheer battle weariness.
Then, this aching schism
arises and demands a fusion of all parts.
How could I acquiesce and comply
and daily deny this vital part of me?
The very Seal imprinted upon every cell
of the new creation of my being?

I awake from my stupor,
when the pain of denial becomes too great,
only to realize that this kind of suffering
is far greater than the occasional blows
that come from standing out from the rest.

August 1994

To contact author for your feedback or any questions relating to her books or to order further published books, please visit **http://piahorangross.com.**

www.ingramcontent.com/pod-product-compliance
Lightning Source LLC
Chambersburg PA
CBHW042052290426
44110CB00006B/162